Boiling Point

Boiling Point

The
Workbook

Dealing with the Anger in Our Lives

JANE MIDDELTON-MOZ

Health Communications, Inc.
Deerfield Beach, Florida

www.hci-online.com

Publisher: Health Communications, Inc.
            3201 S.W. 15th Street
            Deerfield Beach, FL 33442-8190

Cover design by Lawna Oldfield
Inside design by Dawn Grove

This book is dedicated

to the memory of

Dr. Rudolph I. Moz

and to our family and community

CONTENTS

AUTHOR'S NOTE

Those mentioned in the case examples are composites of many adults I have worked with in my thirty years of clinical practice. The impact of trauma on individuals and communities is frequently similar. Any similarity of examples to specific individuals is only a result of these common characteristics.

TO THE READER

This workbook is meant to be a companion to my book *Boiling Point: Dealing with the Anger in Our Lives.* As you work through some of the exercises, powerful feelings may be evoked. That is normal. When working with triggers and issues of grief and shame which are often the foundation of unhealthy anger, it is normal to feel emotions that you may not usually let yourself feel. If you feel overwhelmed, stop. Seek out the support of health-care providers, a counselor or a significant other. Take your time, go slowly and ask for the support you need. Many people who experience unhealthy anger have difficulty reaching out to others. Disconnection and keeping your feelings locked inside are at the root of unhealthy anger that can keep you stuck.

SECTION ONE

WHAT IS ANGER?

Anger is a word that is commonly used to describe a wide range of emotions. I asked a number of people how they would define anger. Below are two examples of the descriptions given:

A woman, age thirty-two, a housekeeper: "Anger is rage inside you that you can't cope with or deal with."

A man, age twenty-seven, a restaurant manager: "Absolutely no control over a situation. Feelings of powerlessness."

The words these two people used to describe anger were:

- Rage
- Inability to cope
- Out of control
- Feelings of powerlessness

FOCUS ON THE EXPRESSIONS OF ANGER THAT YOU HAVE SEEN, HEARD OR EXPERIENCED AROUND YOU (from significant others, coworkers, family members, neighbors, etc.). WHAT ARE THE WORDS YOU WOULD USE TO DESCRIBE THE ANGER YOU HAVE WITNESSED? (Examples: abusive, hurtful, direct, assertive, etc.)

THINK OF THE TIMES YOU HAVE BEEN ANGRY IN THE PAST MONTH. WHAT ARE THE WORDS YOU WOULD USE TO DESCRIBE YOUR ANGER? (Examples: simmering, loud, tense, direct, cold, etc.)

Given the degree of violence and depression surrounding us every day, it is not surprising that most people attempting to define anger actually use words that describe unhealthy anger. Anger is a *HEALTHY EMOTION*. It is a *WARNING SIGNAL* that something is wrong. Anger is very much like a loyal friend that comes by to visit every once in a while. Anger *ALERTS US* to potential physical or psychological trauma. It *PROVIDES US WITH THE ENERGY TO RESIST EMOTIONAL OR PHYSICAL THREATS*. It aids in our *AWARENESS OF OUR EMOTIONAL AND PHYSICAL BOUNDARIES* and *HELPS US SET PROTECTIVE LIMITS*.

Just as fear signals danger, loneliness lets us know that we need to connect with someone, and guilt makes us think twice before we hurt another's feelings or act against our value systems, anger helps us to survive and can motivate us to make needed changes in our lives.

Anger can also mobilize us to direct our energies toward making much-needed changes in our world when faced with injustices. Consider, for example, Mothers Against Drunk Drivers (MADD) or people who fight for needed legislation regarding child abuse and neglect. Many people who work hard to make the world a healthier place are fueled by anger.

The ability to experience anger allows us to survive. Anger lets us know when we are emotionally hurt, being treated unfairly, in need of protecting ourselves, etc. When we try to deny our anger, bury it, intellectualize it, minimize it or ignore it, we turn healthy anger into unhealthy anger.

For example:

Joyce had recently accepted a position as a receptionist in a corporation. Toward the end of her first week of work, her boss yelled at her, blaming her because he had missed an appointment. She clearly remembered letting him know of the appointment and showed him that the missed meeting had been written in his appointment book. He apologized briefly, adding that it was not sufficient to advise him of an appointment and write it in his book, but she must remind him of the appointment regularly. As the days progressed, similar incidents occurred. Joyce was blamed for late reports, missed appointments and errors in contracts. It appeared that her boss made errors regularly and that every mistake he made was blamed on Joyce. Even though she examined the allegations each time, presented him with a contradictory reality and heard his apologies, she began looking for another job at the end of the first month of her employment. Her anger let her know that the good salary and benefits weren't worth the continual attacks on her self-worth.

THINK OF A TIME WHEN THE ANGER YOU FELT HELPED YOU TO MAKE HEALTHY CHANGES IN YOUR LIFE:

The situation:

What I told myself was:

The feelings I experienced were:

The changes I made were:

THINK OF A TIME WHEN YOU IGNORED YOUR FEELINGS OF ANGER AND RESISTED MAKING A CHANGE:

The situation:

What I told myself was:

The feelings I experienced were:

My choices were:

WE'VE ALL BEEN CAREFULLY TAUGHT

When we are young, we learn by the example of adult role models in our lives. They teach us how to deal with feelings of sadness, frustration, helplessness, anxiety, stress and anger. We learn either how to pay attention to our bodies and respond appropriately to the messages they give us, or how to ignore our bodies and numb out. We learn either how to honor and respect ourselves and our emotions, or how to discount ourselves and ignore our feelings. We learn either how to honor and respect the thoughts and feelings of others, or how to believe there is only one right way (ours) and how to look out for "Number One." We gain knowledge concerning what is important to value and what to dismiss as unimportant. We either learn balance or how to manage as best as we can without balance.

By age five, many of us had already learned—through observation, physical punishment, shaming or having love and affection withdrawn—that anger was not acceptable. In order to learn healthy anger expression, it is important for us to understand what we have been taught about anger.

Erica's lessons about anger:

I only knew one set of my grandparents. I clearly remember what they taught me about anger. My grandfather taught me that anger was something to be afraid of. He expressed anger through swearing and stomping around. He was very impatient, and his anger scared me.

My grandmother, on the other hand, taught me that anger was healthy. She expressed healthy anger. She set limits and boundaries. Expressing anger was okay. Abuse was not.

My mother taught me that anger should be controlled and internalized. She took anger out on her body. She taught me to express only sadness and happiness. Being upset and angry was not okay.

My father taught me that anger was fury to be feared. He expressed anger through throwing stuff around. It seemed like the end of the world when he got angry. He'd break stuff, then get in the car and screech away. He would also talk about divorce. Only the family knew this side of my father. To those outside the family, he was always the "nice guy."

Neighbors and friends of the family all seemed to teach me similar things about anger. Men were out of control with their anger, which was dangerous. Women were not allowed to be angry. There was no room for their anger.

WHAT DID YOU LEARN ABOUT ANGER? WHAT WERE THE MESSAGES YOU RECEIVED FROM ADULT ROLE MODELS? HOW DID THEIR EXPRESSIONS OF ANGER MAKE YOU FEEL? HOW DID YOU REACT TO THE EXPRESSIONS OF ANGER AROUND YOU? (Teaching is not only directed through words. Emotional expression is often taught through body language, what is said and not said, silence, attention or lack of attention, etc. If you were not raised by parents or did not have grandparents, answer the questions using father, mother and grandparent figures. For some of you, older brothers and sisters also influenced your lessons about anger.)

WHAT MY GRANDMOTHER(S) TAUGHT ME ABOUT ANGER:

Teachings:

I felt:

I reacted to these lessons by:

WHAT MY GRANDFATHER(S) TAUGHT ME ABOUT ANGER:

Teachings:

I felt:

I reacted to these lessons by:

WHAT MY MOTHER(S) TAUGHT ME ABOUT ANGER:

Teachings:

I felt:

I reacted to these lessons by:

WHAT MY FATHER(S) TAUGHT ME ABOUT ANGER:

Teachings:

I felt:

I reacted to these lessons by:

WHAT MY EXTENDED FAMILY MEMBERS (aunts, uncles, cousins, etc.) TAUGHT ME ABOUT ANGER:

Teachings:

I felt:

I reacted to these lessons by:

WHAT MY NEIGHBORS AND THE FAMILIES OF MY FRIENDS TAUGHT ME ABOUT ANGER:

Teachings:

I felt:

I reacted to these lessons by:

WHAT I LEARNED IN SCHOOL ABOUT ANGER:

Teachings:

I felt:

I reacted to these lessons by:

WHAT I LEARNED FROM BROTHERS AND SISTERS ABOUT ANGER:

Teachings:

I felt:

I reacted to these lessons by:

What Erica learned to tell herself about anger:

Erica suffered recurring bouts of depression throughout her early life. Her first relationship with a man was with one who was verbally abusive.

"When I was a teenager, I sometimes felt my anger was out of control. I was terrified that I was becoming like my dad. Later, whenever I got angry, I would tell myself to think about it. I would berate myself for my feelings and tell myself I was becoming like my dad. I now realize that I never allowed myself room for my own anger. Instead of acting out anger like my dad, I denied myself the right to feel. I became like my mom. I didn't take it out on my body, I became depressed instead.

"What I tell myself today about anger is that it is healthy to experience anger at times but not okay to lash out at people around me. I now also tell myself that it isn't okay to emotionally beat up on myself. After I was able to examine what I learned and experience the shame I felt every time I experienced anger, I realized I'm not my dad or my mom. I learned not to be afraid of my anger. I learned not to personalize the anger of others and was no longer afraid of my father's outbursts."

Over the next week, pay attention to the messages you give yourself about anger. On the following page, list the messages as well as your responses.

(Example: Erica)

Messages	Responses
If I get angry, I'll be like my dad.	I rationalized and intellectualized my angry feelings, then had a two-day bout of depression.

MESSAGES I GAVE MYSELF ABOUT ANGER THIS WEEK:

My Responses:

Erica realized that she had been operating on several myths about anger:

- Anger is an unhealthy emotion.
- Anger, if expressed, is hurtful and dangerous.
- Men express anger and women don't.
- Men can't control their anger.

WHAT ARE SOME OF THE MYTHS YOU HAVE LEARNED ABOUT ANGER WHICH HAVE INFLUENCED YOUR BEHAVIOR?

Emotional competence does not come from hiding or ignoring feelings. Everyone has feelings. Healthy people experience a full range of feelings: joy, anger, sadness, relief, love. Competence comes in acknowledging these feelings for what they are—feelings—and realizing that they can be expressed in healthy ways rather than denied or used to manipulate, bully or control others. Because many of us have learned myths about anger, we don't consider anger as that "good friend" which stops by on occasion to warn us that we may need to make different choices, set boundaries, protect ourselves emotionally and physically, etc.

Consider the example of the difficult boss whom Joyce confronted in the beginning of the chapter. Joyce's anger allowed her to act in her own behalf, removing herself from an emotionally abusive environment. What might Erica have done in that same situation before she learned to make friends with her anger? She had grown up with a father who regularly abused his family emotionally with his anger. Rather than listen to the lessons her anger was teaching her, Erica might well have joined her boss in blaming herself, rationalizing his behavior and tolerating his abuse. Two against one is never good odds. Without the benefit of anger as a "healthy, observant friend," she may well have stayed in the job, allowed regular emotional abuse and experienced frequent bouts of depression. Erica learned to hide her fears and anger behind masks of rationalization, denial and compliance, causing her greatest survival instinct to become the captive of a painful past.

SECTION TWO

THE MANY FACES OF UNHEALTHY ANGER

Anger is a healthy emotion, yet a majority of people in our society are afraid of healthy anger and are taught from a very young age not to feel it or express it. Many people are socialized to "be nice" and not to "make waves," while others are taught to "fight back" rather than allow themselves to feel normal emotions of vulnerability or powerlessness. Many people hide or deny their anger so effectively that they are not even aware of its role in their lives. Anger has ceased to be a healthy, constructive emotion and has become destructive to ourselves and others, as well as to the ability to build healthy relationships. Anger comes out sideways: hurtful humor, clenched jaws, grinding teeth, procrastination, illness, memory loss, chronic lateness, righteousness, gossip, twitching eyes or a constantly moving leg while "relaxing," chronic irritability over small things, depression, or violence.

Violent people were often taught when they were young that sadness, vulnerability and powerlessness were too painful or were not acceptable. They learned to bypass vulnerable feelings and go directly into rage. Some learned to be bullies. They were conditioned to access their anger and to control others with it in order to get what they wanted. Power and control are often what many children learn from adult role models in their families, on television, in movies or in music.

Sometimes the messages that we receive about feelings as we grow up instruct us to hide our emotions from others and often even from ourselves. We learn to show one thing on the outside while experiencing another on the inside. We learn to present masks to the world that conceal our true feelings.

Sid grew up in a family where children were to be "seen and not heard." He was taught to be "a good, compliant boy." He learned that if he expressed anger, love would be withdrawn for hours and sometimes days. "Mother would slam pots and pans around in the kitchen if I displeased her. If I asked what was wrong, she would just stare at me but wouldn't reply." Sid learned to hide his feelings of anger. He learned to wear a mask that hid his true feelings. Below are illustrations of what Sid learned to show on the outside and the feelings that existed under his mask.

OUTSIDE   INSIDE

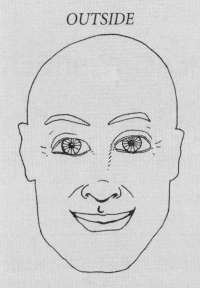 

Sid states that he doesn't get angry. Those close to him disagree. Sid shows his anger by hurtful humor, sarcasm, chronic lateness, and promising things but not following through.

USING THE DRAWINGS OF THE TWO MASKS BELOW, DRAW HOW YOU APPEAR OUTSIDE WHEN YOU FEEL ANGER AND HOW YOU FEEL INSIDE:

OUTSIDE   INSIDE

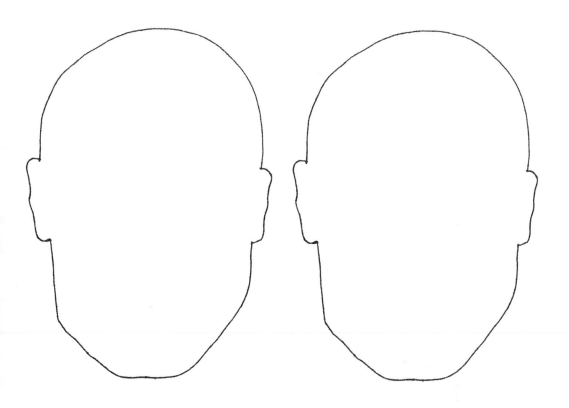

BELOW ARE SOME BEHAVIORS THAT PEOPLE MIGHT EXHIBIT INSTEAD
OF EXPRESSING FEELINGS OF ANGER OR VULNERABILITY. CHECK THE
BEHAVIORS THAT MOST FREQUENTLY APPLY TO YOU. ADD ANY THAT
AREN'T ON THE LIST.

WHEN I AM ANGRY I:
___ tell others that I'm just fine.
___ sulk and pout.
___ feel pain in my body (headache, stomachache, back pain, etc.).
___ can feel my blood pressure rise.
___ become obstinate and do the opposite of what others want.
___ gossip about others.
___ find that others around me become angry at my behavior while I remain
calm.
___ start a fight with someone.
___ become critical of myself.
___ become critical of others.
___ become tense and irritable.
___ seethe inside and sometimes later explode at something which may be
insignificant.
___ avoid the person with whom I am angry.
___ use drugs (including alcohol).
___ store the information and bring it up at other times. I rarely forget about it.
___ become defensive.
___ leave.
___ blame others for my feelings and problems.
___ try to hurt the reputation of the person with whom I am angry.
___ become sarcastic.
___ become cold and distant.
___ don't say anything to the person at the time. My anger comes through
sarcasm and hurtful humor in the company of others.
___ freeze.
___ communicate my feelings.
___ find myself stewing over issues for days.
___ have trouble eating or sleeping.
___ feel discouraged, depressed, moody.
___ punish myself in some way.

____ eat.

____ smoke.

____ portray myself as "having it all together."

____ become silent.

____ throw things or put my fist through things.

____ strike out physically at another (my significant other, children, coworkers).

____ drive aggressively or yell at others on the highway.

____ feel sorry for myself.

____ create fantasies in my mind of how I'm going to hurt others or get back at them.

____ tell myself all the ways the other person is wrong and I'm right.

____ clean frantically.

____ take a break, then communicate my feelings.

____ feel unmotivated.

____ feel the need to be right in order to justify my feelings.

Other examples:

MAKE A LIST OF THE BEHAVIORS YOU HAVE CHECKED.

For example, Sid checked the following behaviors:

Tell others that I'm just fine.

Become obstinate and do the opposite of what others want.

Find that others around me become angry at my behavior while I remain calm.

Become sarcastic.

Become cold and silent.

Promise things and then don't follow through.

MY LIST OF BEHAVIORS (Sometimes it is helpful to check the list out with a friend, your counselor or a support group. Select someone you can trust to give you honest feedback.):

We are frequently unaware that our behaviors form patterns. For instance, there are many styles of anger expression, healthy and unhealthy:

The Fire-Breathing Dragon: Fire-Breathing Dragons use a shield of anger as protection. Anger becomes almost a way of life. These people blow up if others get too close to their personal space. They swear, explode, rant and rave.

The Invisible One: Invisible Ones protect themselves through being emotionally invisible and thereby avoiding any possible conflict or self-exposure. They avoid conflict by giving up independent choice and relying on others to make choices for them. If you ask The Invisible One, "Are you hungry?", the reply will frequently be, "I don't know, are you?" If you ask, "What would you like to eat?", The Invisible One will reply, "What kind of food are you in the mood for?"

The Strategist: Strategists constantly feel controlled from the outside and are frequently angry at this perceived control from others. These people have learned that expressing anger will result in isolation or rejection. They counter the feeling of being controlled by becoming resistant, procrastinating and sabotaging. They will promise the world and then never quite get around to keeping the promises. "I'll do it tomorrow for sure." A Strategist might offer to take you to work, then be late picking you up, or agree to do the laundry only to ruin your favorite piece of clothing. The unknowing object of The Strategist's anger often ends up exploding and expressing the anger The Strategist doesn't express.

The Stamp Collector: Stamp Collectors remember every argument and every perceived slight or injustice perpetrated against them. These people save unresolved conflicts, hurts and issues in their minds like stamps in a book. ("You'll never make up to me for the time you. . . .") The hoarded resentments can serve as protection against further wounds to a vulnerable self. In an argument, the other person will be blasted with every stamp in the book. Or eventually The Stamp Collector will turn the catalog of resentments in on a fully justified divorce, end of friendship, affair, etc.

The Internalizer: Internalizers appear calm on the outside, seemingly going with the flow despite what is going on around them. On closer examination, however, it is apparent that they are only breathing from the neck up and their stomachs are churning like cement mixers. Even though Internalizers might seem to be sitting in a relaxed position, they exert so much physical and emotional control that if you pulled the chair out from under them, they would remain "comfortably" sitting in midair. Anger that is experienced is immediately internalized.

The Righteous One: Righteous Ones might not show outward anger, but instead seethe inside. Frustration and resentment are channeled through the need to be right. Righteous Ones have a need to receive apologies when their "rightness" is questioned. They frequently create dependency in others, then use their suffering as proof of being good and "right." "After all I've done for you, how could you. . . ." The Righteous One needs to be in control at all times.

The Displacer: These people have a fear of people they place in authority (the boss, a teacher, parent figure, etc.). When angry at authority figures, Displacers vent their stored rage on someone else: significant others, children, family pets or some unsuspecting driver on the highway.

The Mine Field: Relating to these people is like walking through a mine field— you never know when you are going to step on the wrong piece of ground and the bomb will go off. Mine Fields are quick to anger and just as quick to forget it. They don't know why those around them act as though they are walking on eggs or are still angry. Those with this style of unhealthy anger expression are explosive and impulsive.

The Whiner: Whining can be regarded as the sound of anger and frustration being forced through a small tube. Whiners complain about the unfairness of it all. They whimper and protest rather than stating their needs or feelings directly.

The Blamer: Blamers take no responsibility for their actions or emotions, but rather blame others for all unfairness, injustices or emotional states. "They made me angry. . . ." "They forced me to. . . ." Whoever "they" are, they are responsible for everything that's wrong if you listen carefully to The Blamer's chorus. They hide their hurt and anger by criticizing others.

The Projector: Projectors attribute feelings, thoughts or mistakes to others while remaining blind to them in themselves. "Joan doesn't like me because I'm over-weight." "Tom's angry at me because he thinks I'm having an affair." In the first case, The Projector is uncomfortable with her own weight gain; in the second case, The Projector is angry and jealous. Projectors frequently accuse others of the anger that they feel themselves.

The Power Broker: Power Brokers do not allow themselves to have feelings of powerlessness, vulnerability or fear. When any of these feelings begin to arise, they are bypassed and immediately turned into rage. The Power Broker must be in control at all times and is frequently violent when feelings of powerlessness or fear are triggered.

The Addict: Addicts turn to drugs or alcohol when they are angry or depressed, or as an excuse to release anger. Sometimes they use drug and alcohol intake as an excuse for rage or aggressive or violent behavior. "You know I wouldn't have hit you if I wasn't drinking."

The Redirector: Redirectors channel all anger energy into tasks. When this type of person is angry, the house gets cleaned or hours of extra time are spent at work. Redirectors can literally hide in tasks and have little time for communication.

The Paranoid: These people are constantly suspicious of the motives or behaviors of the people around them. The Paranoid is usually possessive, jealous and insecure in personal relationships. Anger is mixed with tremendous shame and fear of abandonment.

The Self-Abuser: This person goes a step beyond internalizing anger. Self-Abusers frequently channel anger into self-mutilation. For example, when Self-Abusers are angry, they may cut themselves, hit themselves or injure themselves by hitting a wall. They punish themselves with the anger that is meant for someone else.

The Lateral Oppressor: This type of anger expression is common in those who have been continually oppressed. They can't fight the all-powerful oppressor so they turn their rage and anger on their own group in the form of putdowns, gossip, jealousy, family feuds, competition, gang wars, etc. Examples include women fighting women, Native American against Native American, homosexual fighting homosexual, etc.

The Communicator: Communicators know that anger and conflict are natural and necessary. They have a full range of emotional expression and can communicate concerns effectively. Communicators know how to take on the problem, not attack the person. They can listen attentively and respond from the self rather than attacking. They have the ability to take time and cool off, agree to disagree, compromise, self-examine, make mistakes and apologize when necessary without feeling that the apology diminishes them.

DESCRIBE YOUR STYLE OF ANGER EXPRESSION. (It can be one of those listed on the previous pages, a combination of styles or another style entirely.)

For example:

Sid recognized himself in The Strategist. He realized that the way he was expressing his anger and control was through sabotage and procrastination. He realized that the reason he wasn't "getting around" to his share of the work at home was because he was angry at his wife. He also recognized that his tardiness at work began when he was angry at his boss for increasing his workload with no salary adjustment. Sid also decided that this style of unhealthy anger expression was not working because he was risking both his relationship and his job. He also had recently been depressed. "Hey, I'm not only risking the relationship I have with my wife, but with myself as well."

MY STYLE OF ANGER EXPRESSION IS:

IN WHAT WAYS IS MY ANGER STYLE WORKING TO BENEFIT ME?

THE PRICES I AM PAYING FOR MY CURRENT STYLE OF ANGER EXPRESSION:

CHANGES I WOULD LIKE TO MAKE IN MY STYLE OF ANGER EXPRESSION:

Sid realized that there were benefits to his style of anger expression:

1. *He usually was in control. Nobody could make him do anything.*
2. *He could appear to "be the good guy" while getting his anger out through sabotaging behavior.*

The liabilities, however, far outweighed the benefits:

1. *The distance was getting greater between him and his wife.*
2. *He was on probation at work.*
3. *He was depressed.*

Sid said that he needed the support of his family and others to begin to change his behavior:

1. *He wanted his wife to also recognize her styles of anger expression so they could communicate more effectively. He asked her if she would be willing to complete the workbook. He also asked her to join him in attending a couples retreat sponsored by their church.*
2. *He needed to get his depression under control and had made an appointment with a counselor.*
3. *He needed to confront his boss regarding his workload and asked a friend to go for coffee after work for support.*
4. *He wanted to fix his son's bike that he'd been promising to fix for a month and apologize to him for letting it go. He also wanted to take more of an active role in his son's life, including his discipline.*

ASSISTANCE I WILL NEED IN ORDER TO MAKE THE CHANGES I DESIRE:

MY ACTION PLAN:

SECTION THREE

ANGER TRIGGERS

Frequently anger from our past gets mixed up with anger in the present. When we are feeling more anger than a situation warrants, we can safely assume that we are dealing with past anger which has been triggered by situations in the present.

Each of us should be aware of and accountable for our personal anger triggers—those events that cause us to feel anger. Having triggers is like walking around with a loaded emotional gun inside. Sights, sounds, touch, smells, facial expressions, emotional states, styles of communication, dates, seasons, holidays—even the ages our children turn—can trigger thoughts and feelings from the past that affect our present responses by causing us to overreact, freeze or underreact. For instance, being stuck in a traffic jam might trigger a feeling of helplessness that was experienced at another time of life. For many, helplessness was a feeling that was forbidden, ridiculed or punished. The helpless feeling is bypassed, and the result might be rage.

Many people are underreactors (imploding emotion or shutting down) or overreactors (exploding emotion or acting out). Triggers precede the imploding or exploding of anger or other emotions.

For example:

John was generally seen as "Mr. Nice Guy," yet he would become angry and verbally aggressive whenever he felt helpless, powerless or vulnerable. His triggers might be being stuck in traffic or difficulty with a boss. It is extremely important for John to understand his triggers, so that when they occur he can make choices rather than becoming verbally aggressive with his family or acting out behind the wheel of his car.

ADD YOUR TRIGGERS AND RESPONSES TO THE FOLLOWING LISTS:

Sights   **Immediate Emotional Responses**
Seeing a parent yelling at a child   Sadness
A man in a baseball cap   Anger
Visiting the house I grew up in   Out of control

Sounds	Emotional Response
A baby crying	Rage
A lawn mower	Fear
Yelling	Helplessness

Touch	Emotional Response
Sheets too tight on the bed	Terror
Hair being touched	Rage
Being touched from behind	Rage

Facial Expressions   **Emotional Response**
  Rolling eyes   Rage
  Blank stare   Fear
  Fear   Rage

Emotional States   **Emotional Response**
  Helplessness or vulnerability   Rage
  Anger   Helplessness
  Fear   Rage

Style of Communication
    Lying
    Whining
    Slurred

Emotional Response
    Rage
    Rage
    Numbness

Dates, Seasons, Holidays
    Christmas
    Fall
    June 10

Emotional Response
    Depression
    Fear
    Anger

Ages Our Children Turn	Emotional Response
Age ten	Numbness
Age three	Anger
Age twelve	Fear

When you become aware of anger triggers, you may also learn where the triggers originate. Then you can work on them by deactivating the loaded areas of your life.

John was able to learn a great deal about his anger trigger by outlining the trigger as illustrated in the following charts. This activity involves listing the trigger, the resulting emotional response, the physical response, the behavioral response, the feelings blocked by the behavioral response, and finally the unresolved grief, trauma or shame behind the trigger. Someone may not be able to fill in all of the areas listed. For example, many people know what feelings they are blocking but do not know the unresolved grief, trauma, or shame. Others may know the unresolved grief, trauma or shame but not the emotions blocked.

John's recent triggers:

TRIGGER	EMOTIONAL RESPONSE	PHYSICAL RESPONSE	BEHAVIORAL RESPONSE
Being stuck in traffic	Rage	Sweaty palms, rise in blood pressure	Repeatedly hit the steering wheel and scream obscenities at other drivers
Emotional abuse from boss	Numbness	Neck pain	Sit there and take it
Wife telling me I forgot something at the store	Rage	Rise in blood pressure	Scream at wife

FEELINGS BLOCKED BY MY BEHAVIORAL RESPONSES	UNRESOLVED GRIEF, TRAUMA OR SHAME
Helplessness, powerlessness	Parental domestic violence
Anger	Parental domestic violence
Helplessness, powerlessness	Emotional abuse from boss

Marie's recent anger trigger:

Marie overreacted when her children lied. She had little understanding that her rage response occurred whenever she felt out of control; an aggressive response can block the feeling of vulnerability. Lying wasn't a moral issue, it was a control issue. Marie was going through a messy divorce that she didn't want. Her life felt out of control and had for some time. Besides the triggers themselves and the usual responses to them, she still had to confront the feelings under the response.

TRIGGER	*EMOTIONAL RESPONSE*	*PHYSICAL RESPONSE*	*BEHAVIORAL RESPONSE*
My daughter lying	*Rage*	*Tense, sour stomach*	*Spanking my daughter*

FEELINGS BLOCKED BY MY BEHAVIORAL RESPONSES	*UNRESOLVED GRIEF, TRAUMA OR SHAME*
Vulnerability, powerlessness, feeling out of control	*Recent divorce, death of mother in early childhood*

In order for Marie to take control of her life, regain choice, live in the present and be the nurturing mother she wanted to be, she first needed to understand her anger triggers. The above outline helped her do so.

Mike's recent anger trigger:

Mike would become depressed every Christmas. The pattern was always the same. He would begin shopping in early November, always overspending his budget and running up debts. Early in December he would begin feeling depressed. He would drink more than usual, always alone, and would isolate from friends and loved ones. He would spend Christmas alone, often in bed, refusing all invitations to spend the day with friends. Mike began to understand his behavior when he explored his triggers.

TRIGGER	*EMOTIONAL RESPONSE*	*PHYSICAL RESPONSE*	*BEHAVIORAL RESPONSE*
Christmas	*Depression*	*Tired, numb, no appetite*	*Overextending budget on gifts, drinking and isolating*

FEELINGS BLOCKED BY MY BEHAVIORAL RESPONSES	*UNRESOLVED GRIEF, TRAUMA OR SHAME*
Anger	*Early poverty, father's alcoholism*
	Father's violent behavior on Christmas

REVIEW THE ANGER TRIGGERS AND EMOTIONAL RESPONSES YOU LISTED EARLIER. ADD "PHYSICAL RESPONSE," "BEHAVIORAL RESPONSES," "FEELINGS BLOCKED BY MY BEHAVIORAL RESPONSES," AND INCIDENTS OF "UNRESOLVED GRIEF, TRAUMA OR SHAME" FOR EACH TRIGGER YOU LISTED.

Some people learned to survive painful grief or trauma by blocking either actual memory or body memory. Actual memories are the facts of what occurred. Body memories are the feelings felt at the time. If you have blocked actual memory, you may have difficulty completing the "Unresolved Grief, Trauma or Shame" section. If you have blocked body memory, you may have difficulty completing the "Feelings Blocked by my Behavioral Responses" section. You can learn a great deal even if one of these areas is incomplete. You may be able to fill the section in at a later time.

TRIGGER	*EMOTIONAL RESPONSE*	*PHYSICAL RESPONSE*	*BEHAVIORAL RESPONSE*

FEELINGS BLOCKED BY MY BEHAVIORAL RESPONSES   *UNRESOLVED GRIEF, TRAUMA OR SHAME*

TRIGGER	*EMOTIONAL RESPONSE*	*PHYSICAL RESPONSE*	*BEHAVIORAL RESPONSE*
FEELINGS BLOCKED BY MY BEHAVIORAL RESPONSES		*UNRESOLVED GRIEF, TRAUMA OR SHAME*	

TRIGGER	EMOTIONAL RESPONSE	PHYSICAL RESPONSE	BEHAVIORAL RESPONSE

FEELINGS BLOCKED BY MY BEHAVIORAL RESPONSES   *UNRESOLVED GRIEF, TRAUMA OR SHAME*

BE AWARE OF YOUR ANGER TRIGGERS DURING THE UPCOMING WEEK.
ENTER THEM BELOW AS THEY OCCUR:

TRIGGER	*EMOTIONAL RESPONSE*	*PHYSICAL RESPONSE*	*BEHAVIORAL RESPONSE*

FEELINGS BLOCKED BY MY BEHAVIORAL RESPONSES

UNRESOLVED GRIEF, TRAUMA OR SHAME

When you become aware of anger triggers and learn where they originate, you may then begin to work on them by deactivating the loaded areas of your life. With awareness, you can choose to react differently.

In *Reclaiming Your Life,* psychotherapist Jean Jensen presents the analogy of driving a car on an icy road. Many people step on the brake when the car begins to skid. Of course that's the worst thing to do because you've lost control. When triggered, many people "step on the brake." They surrender choice and react instead. An important lesson to learn when triggered is to "turn into the skid"; find another human being and talk about what is happening. Sometimes "turning into the skid" involves feeling the vulnerability, the powerlessness and the sadness. When you allow yourself to feel the feelings without necessarily reacting to them, you regain control and put yourself back in the driver's seat.

It is not enough for us to understand our triggers. We must take concrete steps to deactivate them. John, Marie and Mike developed action plans that allowed them to begin to defuse their triggers and regain control of their lives.

John's plan for defusing one of his triggers:

TRIGGER AND BEHAVIOR	*ACTION PLAN*
Rage response while stuck in traffic.	*Cool off before getting into car.*
	Listen to calming music or books on tape when driving.
	Develop a plan for dealing more effectively with my boss.
	Keep a journal at work and at home. Write about my anger and feelings of helplessness before getting into the car.
	Seek counseling. Work toward acceptance of the vulnerability and powerlessness I turn into rage.
	Make an appointment with my doctor for an evaluation of my blood pressure and discuss biofeedback techniques.

WAYS I COULD SABOTAGE MYSELF	GUARDS AGAINST SELF-SABOTAGE
Difficulty asking others for help when I'm triggered.	Talk to a friend now, before I'm triggered.
	Instead of isolating at lunch, eat in the lunchroom.
I will react and get into the car before I defuse my trigger.	Accept invitation to carpool with Jim until I can develop some confidence defusing triggers.

Marie's plan to defuse one of her triggers:

TRIGGER AND BEHAVIOR	ACTION PLAN
Daughter's lying and my screaming and spanking her.	Ask my single-parent neighbor if we can begin helping each other with child care, particularly when time-outs are needed.
	Remove myself from the situation. Write my feelings in a journal rather than acting them out.
	Return to my support group. Be honest with them about my behavior with my daughter.
	Let my daughter know that my behavior is not her fault.
	Ask George to join me in short-term counseling with the goal of working out the feelings that interfere with our ability to effectively co-parent.

WAYS I COULD SABOTAGE MYSELF	GUARDS AGAINST SELF-SABOTAGE
My neighbor will not be willing to exchange child care at needed time-outs, and I give up.	Also ask Aunt Joan for help before approaching my neighbor.
My pride won't allow me to ask George to work out healthy co-parenting.	Focus on my daughter's well-being, not on power struggles with George.

Mike's plan to defuse one of his triggers:

TRIGGER AND BEHAVIOR	ACTION PLAN
Christmas isolation.	Accept invitations to be with people during the holidays. Volunteer to feed the homeless Christmas dinner at the shelter.
	Join the adult children of alcoholics support group that has been listed in the paper.
	Attend the workshop on "dealing with the holidays."
	Work on my ghosts of Christmases past.
	Be honest with my doctor about my depression and medicating it with alcohol.
	Make a decision not to drink during the holiday season.

WAYS I COULD SABOTAGE MYSELF	GUARDS AGAINST SELF-SABOTAGE
Let things slide when I'm feeling good.	Let my friends and support group know of my difficulties during the holidays. Ask them to confront me when I'm isolating.
	Make plans with friends. Sign up at the shelter before the holiday begins. Let my friends know of my tendency to isolate.

ENTER YOUR TRIGGERS AND BEHAVIORS, ACTION PLANS, WAYS YOU COULD SABOTAGE YOURSELF AND GUARDS AGAINST SELF-SABOTAGE.

TRIGGERS AND BEHAVIORS	*ACTION PLANS*

WAYS I COULD SABOTAGE MYSELF	*GUARDS AGAINST SELF-SABOTAGE*

TRIGGERS AND BEHAVIORS   *ACTION PLANS*

WAYS I COULD SABOTAGE MYSELF   *GUARDS AGAINST SELF-SABOTAGE*

AFTER TWO WEEKS, EVALUATE YOUR ACTION PLANS. (Have you followed through on the plans you made? If not, why not?) HAVE YOU SABOTAGED YOURSELF? HOW? LIST ANY NECESSARY CHANGES IN YOUR ACTION PLANS.

TWO-WEEK EVALUATION OF MY ACTION PLAN:

I HAVE SABOTAGED MYSELF BY:

NECESSARY CHANGES IN MY ACTION PLANS:

SECTION FOUR

ANGER AND SOCIAL SUPPORT

M any people today are afraid to help someone who is stranded by the side of the road or to ask a neighbor for help. Many people don't know their neighbors. I have met people throughout the world who feel isolated and disconnected from their families and communities.

Unfortunately, this perceived or real isolation has affected many parts of our lives, including our physical health and our vulnerability to episodes of depression, violence and aggression. Countless studies have shown that poor social support not only increases frustration and anxiety that lead to unhealthy anger expression, but also weakens our ability to survive illness. We frequently isolate ourselves when we most need a human connection.

When exploring unhealthy anger, it is impossible not to realize the role that a sense of isolation plays in creating lives that are out of balance and to become aware of the helplessness, frustration, powerlessness and anxiety which are created by that feeling of isolation. We need each other, yet we seldom truly realize how much.

Debbie's story:

The new year didn't start out well for Debbie. In fact, the first months of the year were proof of the old adage, "Sometimes anything that can go wrong, will go wrong." Debbie was told at the end of the first week of the new year that the company she had worked for for the past five years was "downsizing." Since she had less seniority than many coworkers, she was one of many to be laid off before the end of January. Her car magically stopped running the second week in February. Her roommate announced that she was taking a job out of state and would be moving out at the end of February.

Debbie had been given severance pay and had some money in savings, but not nearly enough to support herself, pay for a new car and pay full rent for her apartment. Her bad luck continued. The second week in March, she found a suspicious lump in her breast while doing a regular breast examination. It turned out to be benign, but it gave her quite a scare until the results of a mammogram eased her mind.

Rather than turning to friends and family for support, Debbie stopped returning calls, withdrew from friends, and would tell people who reached out to her that she was "fine" and "just needed some space." She began criticizing herself endlessly, became confused about simple tasks like what clothes to wear, had difficulty eating, isolated more, was continually exhausted but couldn't sleep and generally began feeling worthless. By the end of March, Debbie was deeply depressed.

Debbie had learned from adult role models in her life not to reach out for support. Instead of seeking out friends and family with whom she could express frustration and anger, she continued to "grin and bear it." During one of the most difficult times in Debbie's life, her only constant companion was a talkative ghost who kept telling her, "Don't bother others with your problems, they have problems of their own."

Ghosts are messages we carry from the past that dictate our actions in the present. Some ghosts inform us regularly that it is not okay to seek support when we are in need, therefore keeping us isolated and stuck. Ghosts hang around giving messages that are designed to keep us withholding and hanging onto our anger. The following are some of Debbie's ghosts:

DEBBIE'S GHOSTS

WRITE IN SOME OF YOUR GHOSTS THAT STOP YOU FROM ASKING FOR AND ACCEPTING SUPPORT AND KEEP YOU ISOLATED AND STUCK:

Whether you isolate behind a wall of hostility or isolate behind a smile, the first step to a healthier life may be finding a person with whom you are willing to take risks and build trust. This person may be your significant other, a family member, an elder, a neighbor, an old friend you haven't connected with in a while, a counselor, a spiritual leader, a family member by choice rather than birth, a support group—anyone with whom you can begin to build a real connection.

People working toward building a healthier life have told me repeatedly that the three most important factors in creating positive changes were: getting feedback from others, having permission to express strong feelings and experiencing a sense of belonging.

Many have found it useful early in the process of working toward emotional and physical health to construct their current "social atom." A social atom is basically a map that represents our social life. It is a diagram that illustrates the nucleus of the significant relationships in our life. Our social atom characterizes the quality of our relationships: those close to us and those more distant, those with whom we have conflict, those who trigger us, or those with whom we share the greatest trust, support and intimacy. It provides us with the opportunity to see ourselves within the context of our support system and helps us determine the degree of social support that we are currently receiving.

Through her social atom (see next page), Debbie illustrated the quality of her social support system during one of the most difficult periods of her life. She shows no one close, several with whom she has cut off relationships and two who trigger her. It is interesting that she shows no one with whom she has conflict.

A solid line indicates a feeling of connection; a jagged line, conflict; a dotted line represents a relationship that is gradually becoming disconnected; and a crossed line symbolizes those that trigger unhealthy anger response (body pain, depression, aggressiveness, rage, passive/aggressive behavior, blaming, righteousness, etc.). The absence of a line indicates indifference.

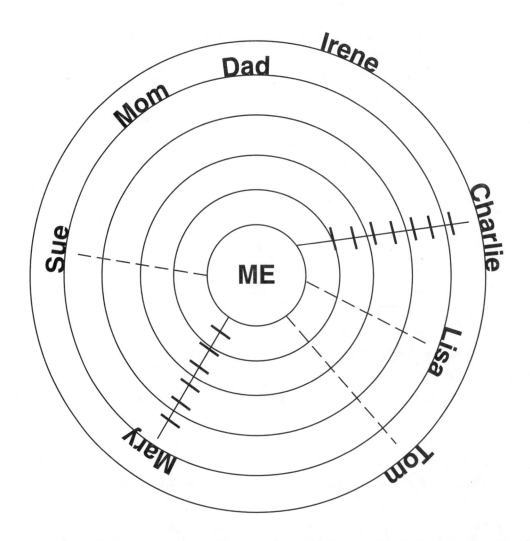

ON THE NEXT PAGE IS A DIAGRAM FOR YOU TO ILLUSTRATE YOUR SOCIAL ATOM. PLACE THOSE PEOPLE IN YOUR LIFE CLOSER TO YOU OR MORE DISTANT, DEPENDING ON THE DEGREE OF INTIMACY AND MUTUAL SUPPORT. SOME HAVE TOLD ME THAT THE DEGREE TO WHICH THEY LET DOWN THEIR MASK WITH EACH PERSON DETERMINED WHETHER THEY PLACED THEM CLOSE OR FARTHER AWAY.

Place a solid line between you and another if there is a solid connection and a feeling of trust; a jagged line represents conflict; a dotted line indicates that the relationship is gradually growing more distant and disconnected; a crossed line represents a relationship where the other triggers an unhealthy anger response in you; and the absence of a line represents indifference. Your social atom solely represents your thoughts and feelings. In some cases people are asked to represent the feelings of both parties on their social atom (for example: Does one person feel close while the other feels distant?). I believe it is important to diagram your social atom illustrating your representation of relationships. This avoids the trap we often fall into of mind-reading.

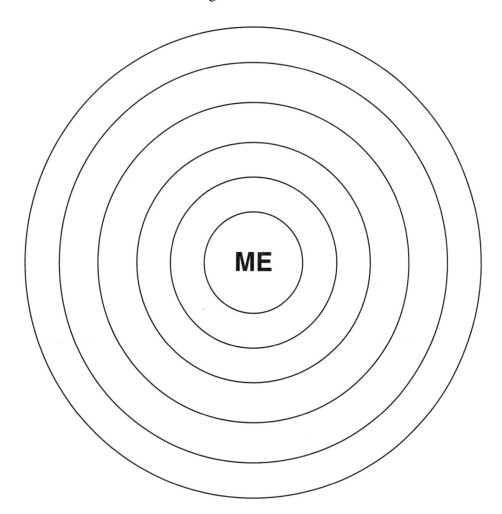

DOES YOUR SOCIAL ATOM REPRESENT A HEALTHY SUPPORT SYSTEM?

WHAT CHANGES COULD YOU MAKE TO STRENGTHEN YOUR SUPPORTIVE NETWORK? WHAT IS YOUR TIME FRAME?

RELATIONSHIP	I WILL	TIME FRAME
(Example) Mary	Call her	Every Monday night for a month

RELATIONSHIPS I WISH TO DEVOTE TIME TO:

RELATIONSHIP	I WILL	TIME FRAME

As you begin to connect with others, share your frustrations, build mutual support and honesty, learn healthy skills in conflict, and build trust, be sure to take note of your ghosts. For every harassing message from a ghost, there needs to be a message overriding the power of the ghost and empowering your goals for change.

The messages Debbie created to disempower her ghosts:

HARASSING MESSAGE	DEBBIE'S RESPONSE
They have enough problems without mine, or *They're too busy right now.*	*I will respect my friends and family enough to trust them to make decisions. I will not read their minds.*
They'll think I'm too weak to deal with my own problems.	*All people need support occasionally. Asking for support is a sign of emotional health, not weakness.*
Grin and bear it.	*Grinning and bearing it doesn't work for my adult role models (they all have health problems) and it hasn't worked for me. This myth has supported my depression, not my health.*
They'll think I'm too weak to deal with my own problems.	*Asking for support is strength, not weakness. Instead of "mind-reading," I'm going to start checking out my judgments.*
Who wants a sad sack for a friend? or *I can handle it myself. It doesn't help to start being dependent.*	*My willingness to be there for others and not allow them to be there for me has created unequal relationships. My lack of willingness to reach out has continued distrust. I'm equal, not superior.*

REVIEW THE HARASSING MESSAGES FROM THE GHOSTS IN YOUR LIFE THAT HAVE KEPT YOU ISOLATED AND STUCK. CREATE NEW MESSAGES THAT WILL EMPOWER YOU IN FOLLOWING THROUGH ON YOUR DECISIONS AND YOUR MOVEMENT TOWARD EMOTIONAL AND PHYSICAL HEALTH.

HARASSING MESSAGE	*HEALTHY RESPONSE*

SECTION FIVE

GRIEF AND ANGER

Loss and the feelings of sadness and sorrow it evokes are an integral part of life. The collection of feelings that loss evokes is called "grief." Some of the normal emotional reactions experienced in grief are: shock, becoming numb, denial, protest, intense and inconsolable sadness, guilt, despair, yearning, helplessness and anger.

One of the most difficult times of my life was when my husband was dying. I remember at one time stomping my feet, feeling frustrated, helpless and angry that Rudy was dying and I would no longer have him in my life. I knew I would miss him desperately.

Anger is a normal part of the process of grieving. Because I was in the embrace of a loving community, I experienced normal grief, including anger. The community that surrounded our family was made up of individuals who encircled us with love and support through Rudy's death and through one full cycle of seasons of grieving.

There are many types of loss that one can experience: death of a loved one, separation and divorce, abandonment, job, family pet, home, safety, security, health, a physical function, etc. When a loss is suffered, there are a number of normal and healthy stages in the grieving process: numbing; denial and partial release; guilt; anger; regression; withdrawal and sadness; social sharing; acceptance; and regaining hope, energy, connection with others, and present and future focus.

Sometimes a person can become stuck in an early stage of grief (numbing, denial, regression, withdrawal and sadness, anger, etc.). This often happens when someone has not grieved prior losses, does not have a support system, has been shamed for feeling, or is ambivalent about the individual that is the object of loss; when there are painful circumstances surrounding the death or loss (example: suicide); or when there is an absence of beliefs and practices that support healthy grief, people can stay stuck in unresolved grief for years.

Frank's story:

Frank had been married for ten years when his wife, Joan, left him for another man. Originally, Frank was in denial. He would consistently interpret Joan's behavior (for instance, calling him to let him know of a special event involving their daughter) as an indication that she was just going through a temporary phase and would return any day. For almost a year, Frank acted as if nothing had changed and would tell friends that he was actually proud of himself for the strength of his patience.

Even though Joan would confront him on his behavior, Frank would still speak to her with words of endearment and put his arms around her when he saw her. This phase came to an abrupt end the day their divorce became final and Joan announced that she was remarrying. Frank became enraged. He was verbally aggressive during phone calls and was sarcastic, attempting to humiliate her whenever he would see her.

Ten years later Frank was still blaming Joan for every problem in his life. They shared the same profession, so he would run into her regularly in meetings and trainings. He continued to be sarcastic and emotionally punitive. Frank didn't remarry and rarely dated. When he did, he would surprise his date with endless talk of his ex-wife and how she had ruined his life.

When Frank began to recognize a history of past unresolved grief and understand the roots of his triggers and anger, he learned a great deal about why he became stuck grieving the end of his marriage. He was then able to mourn the relationship and let Joan go. He began to date. Eventually he remarried without the additional company in the form of his ex-wife's ghost.

Frank listed the losses that he experienced throughout different stages of his life (see next page). He quickly learned that if you don't grieve the losses in one phase, you bring them into the next. Frank shaded the losses that had not been grieved.

He then listed the ungrieved losses, circumstances surrounding the loss, his behavior and the behavior of significant others at the time of the loss, the atmosphere that existed at the time, and beliefs and practices that supported healthy grieving.

FRANK'S LOSSES

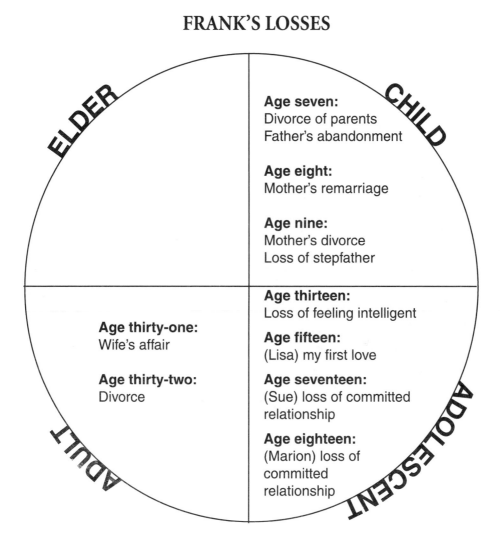

ELDER

CHILD

Age seven:
Divorce of parents
Father's abandonment

Age eight:
Mother's remarriage

Age nine:
Mother's divorce
Loss of stepfather

Age thirteen:
Loss of feeling intelligent

Age thirty-one:
Wife's affair

Age fifteen:
(Lisa) my first love

Age thirty-two:
Divorce

Age seventeen:
(Sue) loss of committed
relationship

Age eighteen:
(Marion) loss of
committed
relationship

ADULT

ADOLESCENT

Three examples of Frank's unresolved grief:

UNGRIEVED LOSSES	*CIRCUMSTANCES SURROUNDING THE LOSS*
Age seven: Divorce of parents	*Dad left when Mother was pregnant with my brother. Mom said he didn't want the responsibilities of one child; two was too much.*
Age seven: Abandonment by Father	*Dad didn't want children. Never saw him again.*
Age seven: Birth of Brother/ Loss of Mother's affection	*Mother attached to my brother and it never was the same between us again. He was the favored child.*

MY BEHAVIOR	*BEHAVIOR OF SIGNIFICANT OTHERS IN MY LIFE*
Begged Father to stay.	*Mother was angry, put him down. Got angry if I said I missed him.*
Felt abandoned but didn't dare talk about my feelings, although I defended him sometimes.	*Mother was angry. Told me he didn't love us. Got angry at me if I said I missed him or defended him.*
Kept trying to gain her approval. Clung to her. I tried to be good.	*Mother said my brother loved her and I didn't, because I loved my dad more and was just like him.*

ATMOSPHERE	*BELIEFS AND PRACTICES THAT SUPPORTED HEALTHY GRIEVING*
Cold and tense	*None*
Cold and tense	*None*
Cold and tense	*None*

Ruth's story:

Ruth was in a severe car accident at the age of nine that resulted in the loss of her sight. Her father was driving the car at the time and was hit by a driver illegally entering the intersection. Ruth was in a coma for several months. Her parents divorced a year later, each blaming the other for the accident. Her mother was supposed to have picked her up from school that day but was delayed at work. Her father stopped to talk to a friend after picking Ruth up at school rather than going straight home. Ruth knew the argument by heart: "If you would have picked her up like you were supposed to, it never would have happened." Or "If you had come straight home, it never would have happened."

Ruth's parents doted on her to the point of overprotection, never allowing her to do anything for herself. She remembered initially trying to talk about the accident and the resulting blindness. Her mother broke down in tears, asking if she could do anything for her, and her father left the room.

Ruth became increasingly helpless and increasingly depressed. She was still living with her mother at the age of twenty-five, having learned few skills to live independently. Ruth's parents encouraged her dependency. If a well-meaning service provider suggested that Ruth begin living on her own, her mother would cry and Ruth would become defensive and angry. "How can you expect me to live on my own, can't you see I'm blind?" Neither parent remarried.

Through work on her depression, Ruth learned that she had never grieved the loss of her sight. As time went on she saw the real "handicap" in her life had been her unresolved grief. "I was never allowed to feel sadness or anger. I could not accept my blindness until I had grieved my loss of sight."

Ruth realized that she had never grieved her parents' divorce and had felt responsible for the difficulty between them. "I actually thought that if I hadn't been hurt, their marriage would have lasted. In a strange way I felt responsible for them."

RUTH'S LOSSES

ELDER

CHILD

Age nine:
Accident—loss of sight

Age ten:
Parents' divorce

Age ten:
Loss of safety
Loss of independence

Ages twenty-one to twenty-five:
Loss of early adult life

Ages thirteen–eighteen:
Loss of sense of self

Loss of independence

Loss of teenage years

ADULT

ADOLESCENT

Ruth's ungrieved losses:

UNGRIEVED LOSSES	CIRCUMSTANCES SURROUNDING THE LOSS
Age nine: Loss of sight	Car accident, parents wouldn't let me talk about loss.
Age ten: Parents' divorce	They blamed each other for the accident.
Age ten: Loss of safety Loss of independence	Parents were overprotective.

MY BEHAVIOR	BEHAVIOR OF SIGNIFICANT OTHERS IN MY LIFE
Tried to talk about my loss of sight.	Mother was angry, put my father down.
I tried not to be too much trouble because I felt responsible for divorce.	Parents hovered over me, wouldn't let me try to take care of myself.

ATMOSPHERE	BELIEFS AND PRACTICES THAT SUPPORTED HEALTHY GRIEVING
Silent and angry Stifling and restricted	None None

WRITE YOUR LOSSES ON THE DIAGRAM BELOW IN THE DEVELOPMEN-TAL SEGMENT IN WHICH THEY OCCURRED:

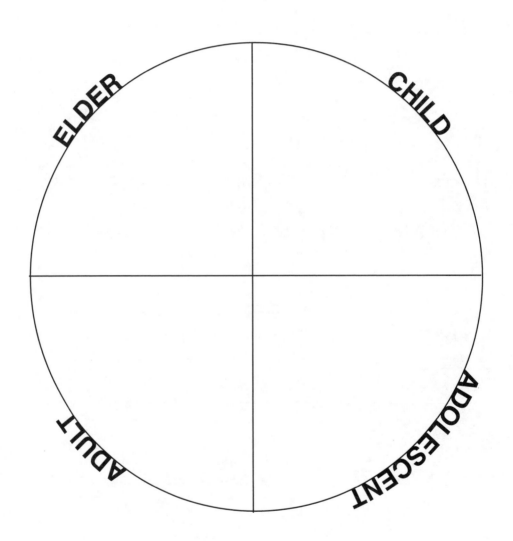

FILL IN THE INFORMATION BELOW:

UNGRIEVED LOSSES

CIRCUMSTANCES SURROUNDING THE LOSS

MY BEHAVIOR

BEHAVIOR OF SIGNIFICANT OTHERS IN MY LIFE

ATMOSPHERE

BELIEFS AND PRACTICES THAT SUPPORTED HEALTHY GRIEVING

When a loss is suffered by an individual, family or community, the most important factor in resolution is connection to others. Three primary reasons for delayed grief are:

1. Lack of social support.
2. Shaming of normal feelings like fear, sadness or anger.
3. Earlier unresolved grief and loss.

It takes one full cycle of seasons to grieve a loss. I was fortunate during that cycle of seasons to have a large community of friends and relatives who upheld meaningful rituals and provided support and understanding to our family.

I remember very little of the week when my husband died. Only now, while involved in preparation for a gathering for the one-year anniversary, am I asking myself basic questions like, "There were a lot of people who stayed at the house. I wonder where everyone slept." Neither my sons nor I remember many of the details of that first period surrounding Rudy's death. I remember not being able to eat or sleep for several days. I recall being sick to my stomach. I remember wandering aimlessly for many days and crying so much that I felt there must not be many tears remaining. I repeatedly relived the last days of his life, wondering if there was anything more I could have said or done. I remember feeling angry at being left.

I was both angry and confused by the seemingly endless number of forms that I had to fill out, and I was amazed by the coldness of some bureaucrats. "Don't they know my best friend just died?" I remember thinking, "Couldn't they have at least said 'I'm sorry for your loss'?"

Gradually my energy increased, and for periods of time the sorrow lessened. Then my sadness would be triggered again by a piece of music, a memory, an anniversary or a holiday. As time passed, the family had many discussions of happy times as well as many humorous memories of our life with Rudy.

If you have ungrieved losses, shame or trauma, it is important to seek out the support of others and, with their help, develop meaningful rituals that can aid you in resolution. We all have needs in the resolution of any loss, be it a loved one, a part of yourself, safety, security, pride in sexuality or the innocence of childhood. We need validation, someone there, modeling of feelings, ritual for grieving and time. Think of the people you can seek out for support and validation. Are there rituals that you can take part in with the support of others which can aid you in the process of letting go of the pain you have carried?

LIST THOSE PEOPLE YOU CAN TURN TO WHO CAN BE SUPPORTIVE IN THE RESOLUTION OF UNRESOLVED LOSS, SHAME OR TRAUMA:

Examples:

A women's or men's support group
Support groups for the victims of trauma
Counselors
Spiritual leaders

THINK OF RITUALS THAT YOU MIGHT PERFORM WITH THE SUPPORT OF OTHERS WHICH WILL AID IN LETTING GO OF PAIN, ANGER, SHAME OR GUILT:

Examples:

I have written a letter to my mother. I don't want to send it. It would help if I could burn it and pray for the strength to let go of my anger.

I would like to have a few close friends come with me to my brother's gravesite. I was little when he died and I wasn't allowed to attend the funeral.

SECTION SIX

ANGER AND SHAME

Shame is a feeling deep within our being that makes us want to hide a part of ourselves from the judgment of others. When we are shamed, we feel inferior, defective, worthless and vulnerable. We lack self-confidence, have poor self-esteem and suffer from endless internal judgments that are evident in continual messages of self-hate. Self-hate is the inclination of people to blame themselves for everything that happens, to see themselves as deficient and deserving of self-abuse and self-castigation. Some people experience constant depression, while others protect a fragile sense of self by projecting blame and hate onto others.

When we are shamed we also feel rage. Shame's constant companion is fear of abandonment. We develop a derivative sense of self: "You're nobody 'til somebody loves you." We become dependent on others for self-acceptance and then angry at those we have empowered to determine our self-worth.

People who practice self-hate subject themselves, as they were once subjected, to an internal tyrant who rarely sleeps and who acts as judge, jury and executioner of the spirit. This inner oppressor judges aspects of the self as bad and in need of punishment if allowed to surface. The shameful parts of the person might include, but are not limited to, anger, vulnerability, fear, sadness or helplessness.

Some learn that to experience anger leads to abandonment, so they never feel safe expressing normal feelings of anger. These people feel anger, followed by shame, debilitating guilt and self-blame. Anger that has not been expressed becomes internalized, causing depression. The inclination of people to self-blame is why Freud categorized depression as anger directed toward the self. Those who are depressed frequently believe they are not lovable, are not good enough and in some cases should not exist. All self-hate is based in shame, the belief that "no matter what I do, I will never be good enough."

Others were shamed for feelings of vulnerability, powerlessness or fear. They learned to bypass these unwanted feelings immediately and explode in hurtful fits of sudden hostility or rage. The slightest perceived criticism or slight will set off feelings of vulnerability, fear, shame and rage. Unfortunately, raging at others in order to hide painful feelings of shame doesn't work very well. Often these outbursts are followed by guilt, fear of rejection and abandonment, and vulnerability—and the shame-rage cycle continues.

Countless people have learned through continual shaming that to make a mistake is to be a mistake. They become hypersensitive to the possibility of criticism from others around them. Once a threat is detected, a loud internal warning signal goes off, and they immediately fight to salvage their fragile sense of self by blaming and criticizing others for unacceptable feelings, thoughts, actions or mistakes.

Many children learn that they must hide entire parts of their being (mistakes, needs, joys, sorrow, sexual feelings, vulnerability, fear, anger, illness, tears) in order to be accepted. Because emotions and needs are normal and healthy parts of any human being, these children grow into adults who continually feel shame. Constantly suppressing a part of one's being requires the child to hide the unwanted part from themselves. Many adults grew up in families that restricted most emotional expression.

IN THE SPACE BELOW LIST THE PARTS OF YOUR BEING THAT YOU LEARNED WERE "UNACCEPTABLE," THE DISGUISES YOU HAVE LEARNED TO WEAR TO HIDE THE "UNACCEPTABLE" PARTS OF YOURSELF AND THE MESSAGES YOU GIVE YOURSELF IN ORDER TO KEEP THE DISGUISE IN PLACE:

PARTS OF MY BEING
THAT I LEARNED WERE UNACCEPTABLE:

Examples:
vulnerability
mistakes

THE DISGUISES I WEAR TO HIDE THE UNACCEPTABLE PARTS OF MYSELF:

Example One:

I look like I can handle anything. I get angry when I feel vulnerable.

Example Two:

I appear competent and am a perfectionist. I need to be right.

NOW WRITE THESE LISTS IN ANOTHER WAY, CHANGING THEM TO RULES THAT YOU HAVE LEARNED TO FOLLOW IN YOUR DAILY LIFE. IN THE SPACE BELOW ADD "I SHOULD NEVER" TO EACH UNACCEPTABLE PART OF YOURSELF AND "I MUST ALWAYS" TO EACH OF YOUR DISGUISES.

RULES I HAVE LEARNED TO FOLLOW THAT INFLUENCE MY BEHAVIOR:

Example One:

I should never allow myself to be vulnerable. I must always act tough. I must be angry when I feel vulnerable.

Example Two:

I should never make mistakes. I must always be competent, perfect and righteous.

Examine the lists of beliefs that you have just completed.

Sometimes, when we examine the beliefs we have learned and continue to believe in our lives, we realize how absurd some of them can be. Would you offer the advice you have listed in the previous exercise to a friend? How much of the advice you give yourself is conducive to health and to forming healthy relationships?

In order to change the beliefs that influence our behavior, it is necessary to examine the shameful messages we have internalized about ourselves and the lessons that we learned about life and the people around us. These early teachings have provided the foundation for the beliefs that influence our behavior. We may have learned that normal anger was bad, it was bad to be vulnerable and have needs, our tears were bad, our thoughts were bad, our normal sexual feelings were dirty, or that we were dirty, unworthy or stupid. We may have learned that people are untrustworthy, judgmental or hurtful.

Psychological injuries not only create wounds, but also result in our putting up defenses against such wounds occurring again. The problem is that we frequently are not familiar with our emotional landscape. So the defenses we have erected might be as harmful in our lives today as they were helpful at an earlier time for our protection and continued survival.

The exercise on the following pages has been valuable for those I have worked with in plotting out their own emotional landscapes. It was developed from the theories of an early psychoanalyst, Alfred Adler, and later Adlerians such as Bernard Shulman (1973).

EXPLORING THE IMPACT OF SHAME

1. In the space below, draw an early memory of shame. The shameful memory could have taken place at home, school, church, community, at a friend's house, in an early relationship, etc. If you feel ashamed to draw a picture because it won't be good enough, it may indicate that you were shamed in art class or perhaps constantly compared to a more artistic brother or sister.

2. When you are finished drawing your picture, think about the child or adolescent and what that young person felt and learned that day. (Think only of the memory depicted in your previous drawing.) Finish the following statements for that child or youth. That day I learned:

I am _____

_____

Life is _____

_____

People are _____

_____

Therefore, I will _____

_____

Example One:

Consider the lessons once learned by this thirty-year-old man. He was recently arrested for domestic violence.

- I am vulnerable, afraid, "a wimp."
- Life is dangerous for those who feel afraid or vulnerable.
- People are critical and judgmental and punish those who are too sensitive.
- Therefore, I will learn never to show vulnerability or fear. I will show that I can be tough and learn to fight. I will never cry again.

Example Two:

Consider the lessons learned by this forty-year-old woman who is currently ending her fifth committed relationship.

- I am unworthy, not good enough to receive the attention of others.
- Life is hurtful.
- People are critical, judgmental and abandoning.
- Therefore, I will attempt to be good enough to earn love and attention. I will be perfect.

DRAWING OF A SHAME MEMORY:

That day I learned:

I am _____

_____

Life is _____

_____

People are _____

_____

Therefore, I will_____

_____

DRAWING OF SHAME MEMORY:

That day I learned:

I am _____

_____

Life is _____

_____

People are _____

_____

Therefore, I will _____

_____

WRITE THE BELIEFS THAT YOU LEARNED ABOUT YOURSELF, LIFE AND PEOPLE:

BELIEFS ABOUT MYSELF	*BELIEFS ABOUT LIFE*
Example One:	
I am vulnerable, afraid and a wimp.	*Life is dangerous for those who feel fear and vulnerability.*
Example Two:	
I am unworthy, not good enough to receive love and attention.	*Life is hurtful.*

BELIEFS ABOUT PEOPLE

Example One:

People are critical, judgmental and punishing.

Example Two:

People are critical, judgmental and abandoning.

Do you still believe the perceptions of yourself, people and life that you formed from your history of shame? Are you still practicing all the "therefore, I wills"? Chances are if you haven't changed your perception of yourself, you haven't changed your survival adaptation—your rules. Children who learned that they were bad, that life was hurtful and that people were judgmental might have survived by learning to be invisible, run, be righteous, rebel or defend against attack with a fire-breathing dragon. We have literally millions of stored memories; they may be full of shame, pride, self-disgust, admiration or a variety of other feelings. Through each experience, we learned more about ourselves, life and people. We also learned how to move through life, rules for behavior, and the beliefs we tell ourselves in the form of constant self-talk that supports and continues our behavior. When we understand the beliefs we carry about ourselves and others, we can begin changing the negative messages we give ourselves.

It's important to understand that the words we use on ourselves came from somewhere. As self-defeating self-talk changes, so do our self-defeating rules and resulting behaviors.

RESPONSES TO SELF-DEFEATING MESSAGES ABOUT MYSELF:

IN THE SPACE BELOW, BEGIN TO COUNTER THE MESSAGES YOU HAVE LISTED ABOUT YOURSELF, LIFE AND PEOPLE. THEN REWRITE THE RULES THAT HAVE SUPPORTED YOUR SELF-DEFEATING BEHAVIORS:

Example One:

   I am vulnerable and afraid sometimes. These are normal and healthy human emotions. Experiencing them is a sign of health.

Example Two:

   I am worthy of receiving love and attention just as I am. I don't have to be perfect. I'm human. There is no such thing as perfection.

RESPONSES TO MY SELF-DEFEATING MESSAGES ABOUT LIFE:

Example One:

I was shamed for expressing vulnerability as a child. I am now an adult and have learned these feelings are healthy and normal. If people have difficulty with my fears or vulnerabilities, I will not personalize their difficulties. I will confide in others instead.

Example Two:

Sometimes life is hurtful, and it is necessary for my well-being to allow myself to feel hurt at times. Life can also be joyous and fun. By cutting off feelings of hurt, I have also not allowed myself the freedom to enjoy life.

RESPONSES TO MY SELF-DEFEATING MESSAGES ABOUT PEOPLE:

Example One:

Some people are critical, judgmental and punishing. They are acting out of their own pain. I won't personalize their behavior. I will learn the difference between supportive, positive feedback and abusive criticism. I will ask those who are shaming to stop. If they won't, I will remove myself from their proximity.

Example Two:

Some people are critical, are judgmental and will leave. I will not personalize shaming behavior. I will accept helpful feedback but not shaming. Abandonment can only happen in childhood. As an adult I am sad when people I love leave, but I am left, not abandoned. There may be ways that I push people away. I need to look at that behavior and stop setting up rejection. If people leave, I will allow myself to grieve.

NEW RULES FOR BEHAVIOR TO REPLACE SELF-DEFEATING RULES:

Example One:

I will express fear and vulnerability when I feel them. It is healthy to experience and express all human emotions.

Example Two:

I will make mistakes like everyone else. I don't need to deny them or defend them. I can learn from the mistakes I make.

SECTION SEVEN

ANGER AND LEARNED HELPLESSNESS

One theoretical explanation for depression, anxiety, aggression and many anger-related illnesses is learned helplessness. This can have significant implications in today's out-of-balance world. A great deal of research suggests that someone's perceived control over one's own experiences produces heightened self-esteem and guards against anxiety and depression. The depressed person, for instance, has learned a degree of helplessness and that any action taken on one's own behalf is futile. Depressed people often perceive that success is not determined by skills, actions, behavior, effort or performance.

Many of us know children who are given what they want without working for it. They, too, develop a form of learned helplessness. These children are conditioned to understand that they will receive what they want regardless of their behavior, actions, abilities or effort.

Martin Seligman and other researchers (1975) conducted experiments which show that when a subject has experienced repeated uncontrolled trauma, the motivation to escape decreases and is replaced with anxiety and depression. Other research studies indicate that uncontrollable rewards also impair motivation and cause a state of learned helplessness that leads to depression. Summarizing such studies, Martin Seligman suggests that "to the degree that uncontrollable events occur, either traumatic or positive, depression will be predisposed and ego strength undermined. To the degree controllable events occur, a sense of mastery and resistance to depression will result." (Martin Seligman, *Helplessness: On Depression, Development, and Death* [New York: W. H. Freeman and Company, 1975], 99)

Through my travels, I meet countless people who tell me they feel that their lives seem out of their control. I remember one man I encountered who was kicking a bank ATM machine. When he saw me he became embarrassed and commented, "I know I just made a fool of myself, but you see it doesn't seem to matter what I do anymore. Computers are in control. Have you ever tried to talk to a computerized voice? What I do doesn't seem to make a difference."

Perhaps runaway technology (as in the case of the ATM), increased psychological trauma, and a perceived chasm between governments and the people who are governed can, at least in part, account for symptoms such as road rage and sky rage. What is certain is that the link between unhealthy anger expression, depression, illness, anxiety and learned helplessness—and the increase in all these—is becoming more obvious.

BELOW IS A LIST OF SITUATIONS THAT FREQUENTLY TRIGGER A SENSE OF HELPLESSNESS IN PEOPLE. CHECK THE ONES THAT APPLY TO YOU.

ADD TO THE LIST ANY OTHER SITUATIONS THAT APPLY.

___ Being confronted with a phone menu when trying to access information.

___ Being stuck in traffic.

___ Your baby is crying and won't stop.

___ You are cut off on the highway by another driver.

___ Your computer goes down.

___ Being robbed.

___ A telemarketer calls.

___ Your neighbor's dog won't stop barking.

___ Your significant other doesn't pick up his or her clothes.

___ Your ride to work is consistently late.

___ A coworker gossips about you.

___ You are confronted with a hostile service provider.

___ You wait for a promised phone call from someone you're interested in.

___ You learn that you have a chronic illness.

___

___

___

___

Knowing our triggers, seeking support, knowing that we are responsible for our behavior and recognizing that we always have choices are the best methods to change learned helplessness into empowerment. The most important consideration in making choices is asking yourself how your choice will affect your safety and the safety of others, and how it will contribute to the physical and emotional well-being of yourself and those dependent upon you for their care.

LIST THE SITUATIONS YOU HAVE CHECKED THAT TRIGGER FEELINGS OF HELPLESSNESS. LIST THE CHOICES YOU HAVE NEXT TO EACH SITUATION. ASK FRIENDS TO HELP YOU CONTINUALLY ADD NEW CHOICES TO YOUR LIST. WE MAY NOT HAVE CONTROL OVER MANY SITUATIONS IN OUR LIVES, BUT WE ALWAYS HAVE THE CHOICE OF HOW TO RESPOND TO THEM.

SITUATION	*MY CHOICES*
Example One:	
My baby is crying and won't stop.	*Check to make sure she is not wet, hungry, running a fever, etc.*
	Remember that many babies have difficulty with their digestive system early on that usually disappears at three months.
	Tell myself that my baby crying doesn't mean I'm a bad parent. It's not personal.
	Ask myself if I'm being triggered. (Am I overreacting?) Ask for assistance working on my triggers. In the meantime, call Joan for some emotional support.
	Ask my partner to take a turn comforting her while I take a walk, exercise, relax.
	If my partner is not available, call on Mom or Auntie Sue for assistance.
	If Mom or Auntie Sue are not available, call one of my friends, Janice or Tony, to relieve me for a bit.
	Ask my doctor and naturopath for suggestions that might relieve her discomfort.

If I am feeling triggered or exhausted and no one can come, try some methods that I've learned can work for both of us: Put her in her carrier and take a walk; take her for a drive, the car's movement sometimes helps her sleep.

Example Two:

A driver cuts in front of me on the highway, then slows down, I pass, he speeds up again.

Pull over, take a breather, get some space between him and me. Nothing is more important than my safety.

Keep remembering that it isn't personal.

Getting home a few minutes later is not that important in the broader scheme of things.

Turn the music on and sing along. It often helps me vent.

Tell myself, "He's a person, too." He has a life, too, complete with problems and frustrations.

SITUATION   *MY CHOICES*

SITUATION	*MY CHOICES*

SECTION EIGHT

ANGER AND YOUR BODY

WHAT IS YOUR BODY TELLING YOU?

Those who have anger-related illnesses are often disconnected from their bodies; that is, they are not aware of what their body is saying to them through various symptoms and reactions. Those who disconnect from their bodies frequently don't know when their blood pressure is rising, their pulse is racing or hydrochloric acid is dumping into their stomachs. Most have no idea even when they are getting angry. As a result they seethe for days, hold grudges, displace their anger inappropriately on their families, rage at drivers, have stomachaches and headaches, grind their teeth, smoke cigarettes, drink alcohol to excess, eat half of a chocolate cake in the space of a few hours, etc. All these actions are meant to displace or postpone one's feelings.

Knowing your body means learning to be a good detective. "My lower back is beginning to hurt. I wonder what happened before it started hurting." Being a good detective means paying attention, which can be difficult when caught up in the details of day-to-day living. Keep a journal that is small enough to fit in a pocket or purse. Use it to record changes in your body that you are aware of during the day. Sometimes you won't be able to make the connection between body pain and triggers right away, but eventually you'll see a pattern begin to form.

I have asked some people to draw an outline of their body (like those shown on the following three pages) in their journal and use colored pencils to shade in areas where anger has settled during the day. For example, through the drawings in her journal, a woman was able to become aware of an important anger trigger. She discovered that she had shaded in red her lower back and stomach areas each time she had contact with a particular friend. Her friend, she became aware, was very controlling and critical, frequently giving unsolicited advice. The woman had never acknowledged her anger at her friend's behavior, but had experienced pain in her stomach and lower back with every interaction. She was eventually able to establish clearer boundaries with her friend. The pain in her stomach and back stopped.

Some of us carry memory of trauma in our bodies (body memory). As stated earlier in this workbook, whenever a trauma happens, we have memory of the event—actual memory. We also have the memory of feelings experienced during the trauma—body memory. Some people block actual memory in order to survive. "I can't remember anything before I was ten." Others block body memory. "When I talk about it, I should be feeling something. It feels like I'm talking about someone else's life."

Louis was brutally physically abused as a child. His father would often hit him on the side of the head or across the legs with his fist or extension cords. Beatings would become particularly vicious when he "talked back."

Louis was in a relationship with a woman who was very controlling and emotionally abusive. When Louis would begin to stand up for himself, he would experience sharp pains in his legs or on the left side of his head. When he began keeping a journal, he became aware that standing up for himself would trigger body pain.

Below is Louis's drawing:

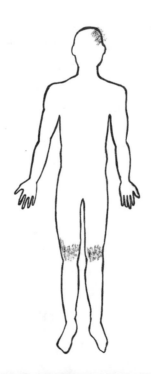

BE A DETECTIVE DURING THE NEXT WEEK. SHADE IN THE AREAS ON THE DRAWING WHERE YOU EXPERIENCE BODY PAIN. USE A CRAYON OR COLORED PENCIL OF A PARTICULAR COLOR TO DO THE SHADING. ALWAYS SHADE IN THAT COLOR. AFTER YOU HAVE IDENTIFIED THE AREAS OF PAIN OR NUMBING, WRITE WHAT YOU WERE DOING, FEELING OR EXPRESSING BEFORE THE PAIN BEGAN.

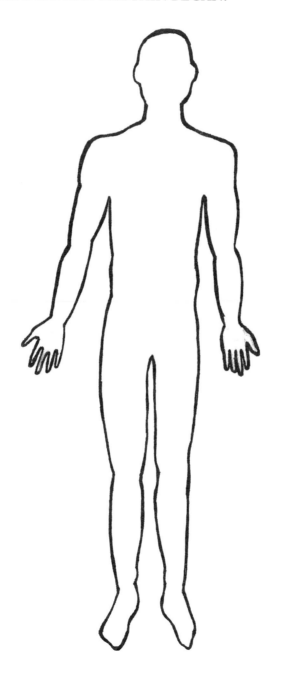

WHAT WAS HAPPENING BEFORE THE PAIN OR NUMBING BEGAN (what was I doing, feeling, who was I with, etc.?):

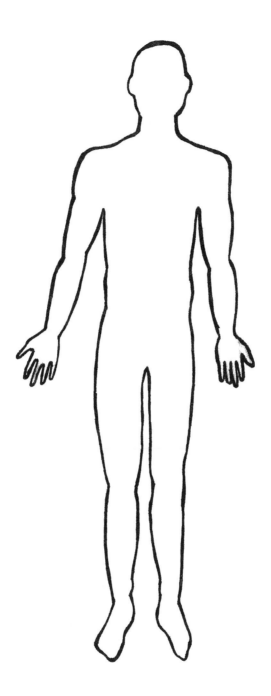

WHAT WAS HAPPENING BEFORE THE PAIN OR NUMBING BEGAN?

There is no substitute for good medical care. Be certain you have a complete physical exam when you first experience body pain or numbing. Make your physician an ally in your healing.

Knowing your body means taking time to focus—taking a few minutes several times a day to allow your body to speak to you. Biofeedback has proven very useful to many individuals with anger-related illnesses. Biofeedback frequently uses machines that provide visual or auditory signals regarding physiological reactions. You might learn to predict an oncoming migraine headache by the cold temperature of your hands. Warming the hands may reduce the intensity of the headache. Another person might experience neck or skeletal pain whenever standing in front of a group of people. Your doctor might be able to refer you to someone who practices biofeedback techniques.

Your physician might also suggest other useful ways to become more aware of what your body is saying. Speak honestly and directly to your physician about your concerns and your decision to become more aware of the effects that unhealthy anger is having on your body.

IS YOUR LIFE IN BALANCE?

One of the most important factors in physical and emotional health is living a life that is in balance. Many years ago, Harold Belmont—a Native American elder, spiritual leader, trainer and consultant—taught a useful tool that helps people regularly evaluate the degree of balance in their lives. The tool is based on the centuries-old Native American medicine wheel.

There are four quadrants on the wheel: mental, emotional, spiritual and physical. For the purposes of self-evaluation, Harold instructed that each of the four lines which separate the quadrants be broken into ten segments. The idea is to evaluate oneself in each area, starting at the center and moving out. For instance, if you spend a great deal of time in mental activity (reading, school work, working on a computer or intellectualizing), you might rate yourself high mentally, perhaps an eight. You would therefore put a dot on the eighth space on the quadrant line relating to mental.

Before undertaking the task of evaluating yourself, further definition in each area might be useful:

Mental

The time you spend in mental activity. Mental focus globally has resulted in a great deal of technological advancement.

Emotional

Achieving emotional balance means the ability to experience an entire range of emotional expression. Those who have emotional competency can allow themselves to be dependent sometimes as well as being independent. They experience their emotions in the present. They cry when they are sad and laugh when they are happy. They have a sense of humor. Emotionally competent people express anger productively rather than in ways that are destructive to themselves or others.

When evaluating yourself, you might ask: "Do I smile when I am angry or sad? Do I become rageful or hostile when I feel vulnerable? Do I cry when I'm really angry? Am I always gloomy or do I have equal periods of joy? Do I blame others when things go wrong? Do I allow myself to make mistakes? Are there long periods of time when I feel numb?"

In evaluating yourself in this area, you might consider whether you are in a period of growth or if you've been at a standstill for a while. For instance, a person might spend a great deal of time going to support groups or going to counseling, yet may be stuck in anger after years of focus on emotional health. That same person may have said that they've "forgiven" an abuser early in their personal work, yet may still feel pain in their stomach every time they encounter the abuser.

Social/Cultural

Social/cultural competency means connection. Do you feel connected with others or do you feel isolated? Are you active in your community? Do you feel a connection to your cultural heritage? Do you feel comfortable giving and being given to? Do you spend time alone as well as with others? Do you feel comfortable asking for what you need as well as responding to the needs of others?

Physical

Living in physical balance means paying attention to your body. For example: Are you sick more than you're healthy? Do you drink alcohol to excess? Do you smoke? Do you use drugs? Do you exercise? Do you eat foods that help or foods that harm? Is your diet balanced? Do you maintain a weight that is healthy for you? Do you sleep well or do you awaken tired? Do you practice preventive health?

Belmont suggests that it is useful to evaluate yourself and also have a friend evaluate you on a separate piece of paper. The person you choose might also perform a self-evaluation and have you evaluate her or him. The person you select should be someone who knows you well and will not have difficulty giving you honest feedback.

After you and your chosen partner in this exercise have evaluated yourselves and each other, share your perceptions. After you have marked each area, connect the markings. Does it make a circle? Are you in balance or is your life out of balance? Does your perception of yourself agree with that of your partner? What have you learned?

Below is a life out of balance:

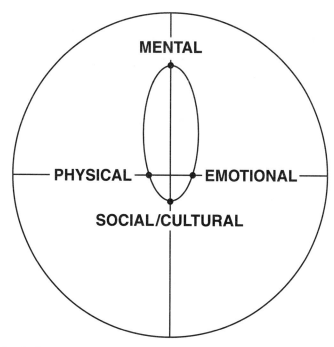

Below is a life in balance:

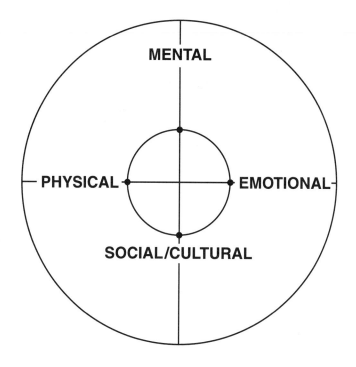

EVALUATE THE BALANCE IN YOUR LIFE:

HAVE I BEEN IN BALANCE THIS WEEK?

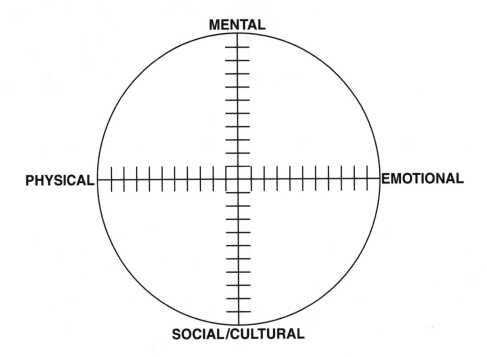

HAVE I BEEN IN BALANCE THIS WEEK?

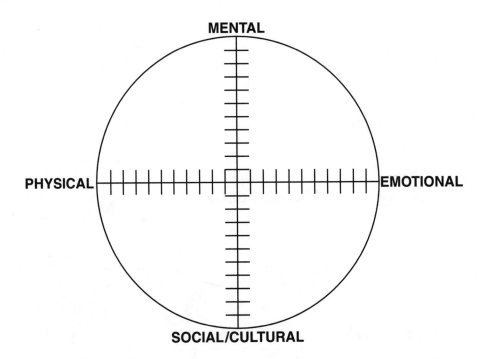

HAVE I BEEN IN BALANCE THIS WEEK?

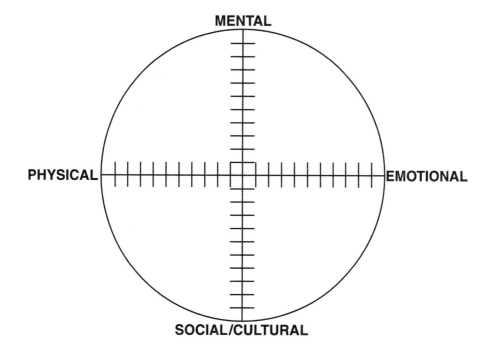

WAS YOUR LIFE IN BALANCE? IF NOT, DEVELOP ACTION PLANS TO BEGIN TO BE IN BALANCE:

ACTION PLAN:

SECTION NINE

UNHEALTHY ANGER IN RELATIONSHIPS

Contrary to popular thought, relationships aren't always made in heaven. Each person comes into the relationship with personal luggage—complete with a trunk full of myths, triggers, ghosts, needs (healthy and not so healthy), and styles of dealing with conflict and anger.

Many relationships are built on foundations of unrealistic beliefs or myths. We frequently blame our significant other when the fiction touted in old movies and television shows doesn't materialize, even though we grew up in very real families that taught us these myths were hogwash. When was the last time you came home to find your partner, wearing a dress and high heels or a suit and tie, clamoring to meet your every emotional need? On one level we know we don't live in "Pleasantville." Yet, on another level, we sometimes blame our significant other when it doesn't materialize.

If we listen carefully to the words of many love songs that have set the stage for intimate moments throughout history, we hear the same myths reinforced regularly: "I can't live without you," "I'm lost without you," " You are my world." The difficulty is that on a very basic level many of us have come to believe these myths, then are frustrated, disappointed and angry when our very real relationships don't match the myth. For example, two common relationship myths are: our love will change our partner into the person of our dreams; and our significant other will fill all of our needs.

THINK CAREFULLY ABOUT THE WORDS THAT HAVE BEEN EXCHANGED IN RECENT ARGUMENTS WITH YOUR SIGNIFICANT OTHER. ARE THERE UNDERLYING MYTHS THAT SEEM TO SERVE AS THE FOUNDATION FOR THESE CONFLICTS? ADD YOUR MYTHS TO THE LIST BELOW.

RELATIONSHIP MYTHS

My partner should know my needs without me stating them.

My partner should make me happy.

My partner will change if I love him or her enough.

REALISTIC EXPECTATIONS OF LOVE RELATIONSHIPS

NOW WRITE REALISTIC EXPECTATIONS TO REPLACE UNREALISTIC MYTHS:

Each individual in a relationship is responsible for clearly communicating needs. It is not up to my partner to read my mind.

Each individual in a relationship is responsible for his or her happiness. A sense of happiness and well-being comes from the inside, not the outside.

I do not have the capability to change another, only myself. It is my responsibility, when making a commitment to a relationship, to partner with a real person and not the fantasy person I want her or him to become.

In many relationships, partners trigger each other in spirals that rapidly escalate out of control. Consider the relationship between Alex and Sue:

A dangerous escalation—Alex and Sue:

In the beginning of their relationship, Alex and Sue were together constantly. They met at the office, quickly moved in together and married six months later.

Alex talked frequently about his childhood. He said his parents had little time for him. Sue was determined to make up to Alex for all the love and attention he had missed. She originally pampered him and made allowances for his moods. As time went on, however, she began to be angry at his lack of appreciation. By the beginning of their second year of marriage, regular arguments consisted of each blaming the other for their unhappiness. Alex accused Sue of "ignoring his needs just as his parents had." Sue accused Alex of being "ungrateful for all she'd done."

In their third year of marriage, Sue decided to return to school to work on her master's degree. This meant she was gone many evenings. Shortly after beginning classes, she began noticing that Alex would sometimes come home late as well. When she confronted him on his late hours, he originally became defensive, then told her he was having an affair. Alex said he didn't love the woman but that he was terribly lonely. Sue became enraged, insisting on knowing every detail of the affair. For a week, every minute spent together was filled by Sue's questions and Alex's confessions.

A week later, Sue stayed home from work complaining of a stomachache. When Alex came home from work, he found Sue unconscious. She had taken a combination of over-the-counter sleeping pills and the pain medicine Alex had been prescribed for a back injury.

Sue was in the hospital for two days, Alex by her side. Alex promised that he would end his affair. Sue promised to drop out of school in order to spend more time with Alex.

Thankfully, not all couples' arguments spiral to this degree of lethality. After much hard work, Sue and Alex were able to identify their triggers and escalating spiral.

Alex and Sue's spiral:

TRIGGER	EMOTIONAL RESPONSE	BEHAVIORAL RESPONSE
Alex: Intimate relationship	Fear	Clinging, asking Sue to meet my unfulfilled needs
Sue: Alex's neediness	Fear	Trying to meet all his needs, being very "good"
Alex: Sue's gradual withdrawal	Anger	Being irritable, demanding, critical
Sue: Alex's lack of gratitude	Anger	Withdrawing
Alex: Sue gone at night	Fear	Had affair
Sue: Alex's affair	Depression	Suicide attempt

FEELINGS BLOCKED BY BEHAVIORAL RESPONSE	UNRESOLVED GRIEF, TRAUMA OR SHAME
Anger	Emotional abandonment in childhood
Anger	Mother's emotional abandonment due to chronic depression, parents' divorce
Vulnerable, powerless	Parental abandonment, my feelings of not being good enough
Vulnerable, fearful	Trying to meet Mom's needs, not doing it well enough to get her love, her continued depression
Anger	Being left alone
Anger	Mother's depression, Dad's new marriage

Although most couples' power struggles and arguments aren't this extreme, trigger spirals usually do exist when couples have difficulty with conflict and have not deactivated their triggers. The first step in change is recognizing your trigger spirals.

THINK OF YOUR MOST RECENT ARGUMENT AND ILLUSTRATE YOUR ESCALATING TRIGGER SPIRAL BELOW:

TRIGGERS	*EMOTIONAL RESPONSES*	*BEHAVIORAL RESPONSES*

FEELINGS BLOCKED BY BEHAVIORAL RESPONSES		*UNRESOLVED GRIEF, TRAUMA OR SHAME*

RELATIONSHIPS ARE HARD WORK. IDENTIFY THE ESCALATING
TRIGGER SPIRAL IN YOUR NEXT ARGUMENT:

TRIGGERS	*EMOTIONAL RESPONSES*	*BEHAVIORAL RESPONSES*

FEELINGS BLOCKED BY BEHAVIORAL RESPONSES		*UNRESOLVED GRIEF, TRAUMA OR SHAME*

In order to stop trigger spirals from occurring, it is important to make concrete plans during stable times in the relationship to prevent future escalation. Sometimes it is helpful to share your triggers, communicate each of your support needs when triggers become activated, develop strategies to prevent personalizing the other's triggers, and create action steps to take if future arguments begin to escalate.

A contest of suffering—Rachel and Christine:

Rachel and Christine have been in a committed relationship for eleven years. Two years ago, they willingly took on the home-care responsibilities for Christine's favorite elderly aunt, the only family member who had been continually supportive of their relationship. She suffered from crippling MS. The family had made a decision to place her in a home for the elderly when her needs for continual care prohibited her from living alone. Rachel and Christine loved her deeply and wanted to care for her themselves.

They identified escalating trigger spirals in their relationship, which had begun shortly after taking on this added responsibility. They each recognized that the trigger spirals, now occurring regularly in their relationship, were sabotaging intimacy and healthy supportive communication. They also realized that the escalating spirals were undermining their individual efforts toward personal growth.

The first step was to jointly identify the trigger spiral:

TRIGGERS	EMOTIONAL RESPONSE	BEHAVIORAL RESPONSE
Rachel: *Christine becoming tired*	*Fear*	*Takes on more responsibility*
Christine: *Rachel overworking*	*Fear*	*Begins to withdraw*
Christine's withdrawal	*Fear*	*Becomes ill, takes space*
Rachel's migraines	*Feels numb*	*Withdraws further, works harder and stores resentments*
Christine's loud withdrawal	*Depression*	*Sleeps late, ignores Christine when she gets up, reads the paper*
Rachel sleeping late and reading the paper	*Rage*	*Screams at Rachel, then totally withdraws behind a wall of silence*
Rachel's withdrawal	*Rage*	*Threatens to end relationship*

FEELINGS BLOCKED BY BEHAVIORAL RESPONSE	UNRESOLVED GRIEF, TRAUMA OR SHAME
Anger	Father's temper, being super good
Fear	Workaholic mother died of cancer
Anger	Father's explosions after silence, mother being hit
Anger	Mother's death
Anger	Always walking on eggs, time-bomb father
Fear	Mother died in her sleep, took mother's place
Fear	Continued family violence

The next step for Rachel and Christine was to each take their own responsibility for individual triggers and joint responsibility for the escalation of the trigger spiral. Following are examples from the action plan they developed.

EXAMPLES OF SUPPORT REQUESTED BY CHRISTINE

Asked if Rachel was willing to do an equal share of the work, not more or less.

Wanted to be responsible for her own fatigue and to let Rachel know if she needed extra help.

ONE SUPPORT REQUEST FROM RACHEL

Asked Christine if she would be willing to allow her to do a reality check when she saw Christine becoming tired or withdrawing in order to stop mind-reading and making inaccurate judgments: "Do you need me to take on extra work?" "Are you angry, or do you just need space?"

Three Joint Action Plans
to Prevent Escalation of Spiral

1. Christine was willing to work on stating her feelings instead of withdrawing. If she did withdraw, she was willing to agree to talk about her feelings sometime before going to bed.
2. Rachel was willing to work on expressing her anger rather than taking it out on her body. If a migraine occurred, she was willing to discuss her feelings after it was over.
3. Both agreed to obtain outside help once a week in order to go out together.

IN THE SPACE BELOW, EACH WRITE YOUR REQUESTS FOR SUPPORT. REMEMBER, YOU ARE RESPONSIBLE AND ACCOUNTABLE FOR YOUR OWN TRIGGERS. YOU ARE ASKING FOR ASSISTANCE.

My Requests for Support:

My Partner's Requests for Support:

Joint Action Plans to Decrease Escalation of Trigger Spirals:

REMEMBER TO BE AWARE OF YOUR GHOSTS (harassing messages from the past that keep you stuck). FILL IN YOUR GHOSTS. ON THE NEXT PAGE, LIST THE HARASSING MESSAGES AS WELL AS THE RESPONSES YOU CREATE THAT WILL HELP YOU GUARD AGAINST SELF-SABOTAGE IN GETTING THE SUPPORT YOU NEED. SHARE BOTH WITH YOUR SIGNIFICANT OTHER.

MY RELATIONSHIP GHOSTS

LIST THE HARASSING MESSAGES FROM GHOSTS THAT KEEP YOU STUCK. THEN LIST THE RESPONSE YOU CREATE TO EMPOWER YOU IN FOLLOWING THROUGH ON YOUR ACTION PLAN.

HARASSING MESSAGES	*MY RESPONSES*

MY RELATIONSHIP GHOSTS

HARASSING MESSAGES   MY RESPONSES

Two of the biggest roadblocks on the path to creating and maintaining healthy relationships are mind reading and passing judgment. Mind reading is believing you know what another is thinking or feeling without checking it out. "She's angry at me because I asked her to stop by the store." "He doesn't love me anymore." Passing judgment is unfairly evaluating another's behavior, character, feelings or motives. "He's just being kind because he wants something." "She doesn't care about anybody but herself." We try and convict others in our minds without giving them the benefit of due process. Both mind reading and inaccurate judgments frequently heighten angry feelings.

When we realize that we are mind reading, the most important thing to do before we go any further in fantasy is check it out.

For example:

MIND READING	*REALITY CHECK*
He is thinking that I'm stupid.	*Actually, you are one of the brightest people I know. I admire you.*
She's mad because I asked friends over.	*I'm not mad. I think I have the flu.*
She doesn't want me to go with her.	*Actually, I just bought plane tickets as a surprise. I was hoping you could join me for the weekend.*

OVER THE NEXT WEEK, KEEP TRACK OF THE TIMES THAT YOU "MIND READ" AND ENTER YOUR THOUGHTS BELOW. THEN CHECK IT OUT AND ENTER THE RESULTS OF YOUR REALITY CHECK.

DAY	MY MIND READING	REALITY CHECK

When we are insecure, disappointed or angry, it is common to make inaccurate judgments about others. Sometimes it is a way of venting our anger in our minds. "His thoughts are really lame." Sometimes it serves to escalate anger that has been brewing. "I just know she's having an affair. Why else would she be late coming home?" In most cases, judgments are dehumanizing, self-defeating and inaccurate. Passing judgment often escalates our unhealthy anger or the unhealthy anger of others. It is important to add some reality to our unfair evaluations.

For example:

Judgmental Thought: *"He's just staying for the children."*

Fair Assessment: *"That's probably not the case. He loves the children and he lets me know it in little ways all the time. I'm just disappointed that it seems we have so little time together, and I'm feeling bad about myself because I took my frustrations out on him this morning."*

Judgmental Thought: *"She thinks she's so great! Look at her lording it over me!"*

Fair Assessment: *"She's not bragging. She's just having fun. It was only a game. I'm so competitive, I feel like a failure when I lose."*

KEEP TRACK OF THE TIMES YOU PASS JUDGMENTS ON OTHERS THIS WEEK. WRITE DOWN YOUR JUDGMENT AND THEN SPEND SOME QUIET TIME THINKING ABOUT THE EVALUATION YOU MADE AND ADD A FAIR ASSESSMENT.

Day   Judgmental Thought:

Day   Fair Assessment:

Day   Judgmental Thought:

Day   Fair Assessment:

SECTION TEN

ANGER AND OUR CHILDREN

In the nine months between October 1997 and June 1998, fifteen people were killed and forty-two were wounded in multiple-victim school shootings in the United States. On April 20, 1999, still more youths were fired upon by other youths, leaving fifteen dead and twenty wounded at Columbine High School in Littleton, Colorado. The shock for many was that these shootings didn't take place in huge cities like New York, Detroit or Los Angeles. Instead, students opened fire in much smaller areas: Pearl, Mississippi; West Paducah, Kentucky; Stamps, Arkansas; Moses Lake, Washington; Jonesboro, Arkansas. The youths that committed these senseless shootings ranged in age from eleven to seventeen. They weren't gang members or delinquents. For the most part, these kids got good grades and had no criminal records.

In each case, many community members knew the youths were troubled but didn't believe that the end results would be murder, even when the boys warned others of their intentions. One woman questioned, "What in the world is happening to our kids? Why are they doing these senseless attacks on their fellow classmates and teachers?" As horrific as the school shootings have been, it is even more frightening to know that the Children's Defense Fund reports that more than 5,300 children are arrested daily, 237 for violent crimes. Even more children and youths are depressed and suicidal. Hundreds might ask, "What is happening?" A more pressing question might be, "What are we going to do about it?"

Concerns about youths aren't new, but today's types of concern are different. Many parents are telling me that part of their elementary school child's language includes threats of violence. "I'm going to kill you." "I wish you would die." "I'm going to shoot you." These statements are not reserved for peers, but said to parents as well.

Many are looking for simple solutions to a very complex issue. In this section of the workbook, you will have the opportunity to explore lessons that are being learned by your children in three major areas: family and community modeling, desensitization and operant conditioning, and family values. At the end of the section you will find potential warning signs to be aware of in children at risk.

What Are You Teaching Your Children About Anger?

Children learn how to express anger from observing the expressions of anger seen every day in their homes, in their neighborhoods and on the playground. For one full week, be a detective. Keep a journal of the expressions of anger you would see from your child's point of view—in yourself, other family members, neighbors and on the playground.

Example:

Monday:

Sarah witnessed me getting angry at her father and not talking to him at dinner. I was angry at Sarah for not putting her toys away. I yelled at her, then put them away myself. I stayed angry at her and wouldn't read her a story.

LESSONS MY CHILD(REN) LEARNED ABOUT ANGER FROM ME THIS WEEK:

LESSONS MY CHILD(REN) LEARNED ABOUT ANGER FROM ME THIS WEEK:

Other Family Members:

Example:

Monday:

My mom shamed my dad for forgetting the errand he promised to run. Dad walked out and didn't come back for an hour, then wouldn't speak to her or anyone else for the rest of the afternoon.

WHAT MY CHILD(REN) LEARNED ABOUT ANGER FROM OTHER MEMBERS OF THE FAMILY THIS WEEK:

In the Neighborhood:

Example:

Monday:

Sarah and I witnessed a mother hitting her child in the grocery store. Sarah witnessed a neighbor yelling at her child to get in the car, then start to drive away without him.

WHAT MY CHILD(REN) LEARNED ABOUT ANGER FROM NEIGHBORS AND COMMUNITY MEMBERS THIS WEEK:

In School:

Example:

Monday:

Sarah saw two little boys fist-fighting on the playground. The teacher yelled at them and sent them to the principal's office. Everyone had to go in early from recess.

One of Sarah's classmates got angry at her for playing with another little girl and then didn't invite her to her birthday party.

WHAT MY CHILD(REN) LEARNED ABOUT ANGER IN SCHOOL THIS WEEK:

Lessons Learned About Anger This Week:

Example:

Sarah learned that when you got angry at someone, you ignored them or rejected them.

Sarah learned that if you were angry at someone, you hit them.

Sarah learned that if you were angry at someone, others were punished as well.

THE LESSONS MY CHILD(REN) LEARNED ABOUT ANGER THIS WEEK:

Lessons I Want My Child(ren) to Learn:

Example:

I want Sarah to learn that anger is normal.

I want her to learn that you can get angry at someone and work it out.

I want her to learn to talk about her anger rather than hitting or rejecting.

THE LESSONS I WANT TO TEACH MY CHILD(REN) ABOUT ANGER:

Steps to Take:

Examples:

I will talk about my anger rather than walking out or rejecting. If I find myself practicing old behavior, I will talk about it after taking a time-out.

As parents, we will talk about what we want to teach Sarah and work on resolving differences rather than walking out on each other. We have agreed to remind each other what we promised when we slip into old punishing behaviors.

I will talk to Sarah about her feelings with her friend.

I will talk to the teachers at the school about the importance of the children learning conflict resolution skills.

STEPS I CAN TAKE TO TEACH MY CHILD(REN) THE LESSONS I WANT THEM TO LEARN ABOUT ANGER EXPRESSION:

In order to teach our children the lessons we want them to learn about anger expression, it is important for us to be aware of the behaviors in our children that trigger us, how we have responded to our triggers, steps we can take to change our behavior and the support we will need to respond differently.

BELOW ARE COMMON ANGER TRIGGERS THAT PARENTS HAVE TO CHILDREN'S BEHAVIOR. CHECK THE TRIGGERS THAT APPLY TO YOU. WRITE IN ANY ADDITIONAL ONES.

___ My child doesn't do what I tell her or him to do.

___ My child won't stop crying.

___ My child lies to me.

___ My children fight in the car and won't stop.

___ My children fighting.

___ My child won't share.

___ My child won't eat something I've cooked.

___ My child won't do assigned chores.

___ My child misbehaves in stores.

___ My child won't do her or his homework.

___ My child talks back.

___ My child leaves things lying around the house.

___ My child keeps interrupting me when I'm talking on the phone.

___ My child won't answer me when I'm asking a question.

___ My child says she's already done something when she hasn't.

___ My child takes things without asking.

___ My child throws a tantrum over not getting his or her own way.

Most of the behaviors listed on the previous page are "normal" behaviors for children. They are "doing their job," being children. Sometimes they escalate behavior when they are given negative attention. They also tend to escalate behavior when they are tired, are afraid or have eaten too much sugar. It will be important to understand the behaviors that are normal for your child's developmental age. For instance, two-year-olds are just doing their job when they say "no."

It will be important to judge the degree of your reaction to your child's behavior and to add the triggers to the list of triggers you worked on in Section One if your reaction is more than "normal frustration." It is normal for parents to become frustrated at times. When the reaction is extreme, however, you may be "living in another time zone" and will need to follow the exercises in Section One to deactivate the trigger.

It is also important to be aware of the messages you give yourself when you are triggered. (Remember the ghosts.) The messages we give ourselves when our children's behavior triggers us often serve to escalate our anger. For example: Your child doesn't pick up his toys when you ask him to. The message you give yourself is, "He knows better. He's just trying to annoy me." The message escalates your anger.

DURING THE UPCOMING WEEK, LIST THE BEHAVIORS THAT TRIGGER YOU, THE MESSAGE THAT WENT THROUGH YOUR MIND WHEN TRIGGERED AND YOUR RESPONSE TO THE TRIGGER:

Example:

Monday:

TRIGGER	*MESSAGE*	*RESPONSE*
My children fighting.	*They are trying to annoy me.*	*I screamed at them.*
	They don't want me to rest.	*Told them they were trying to drive me crazy.*

TRIGGER	*MESSAGE*	*RESPONSE*

TAKE A FEW MINUTES EACH EVENING NEXT WEEK AND CHANGE THE
MESSAGE AS WELL AS LISTING THE RESPONSE YOU WANTED TO MAKE.

Example:

Monday:

NEW MESSAGE	*HOW I WANT TO RESPOND*
They aren't trying to annoy me, they are being normal children and they wanted some attention after I'd been away all day. They love me just like I love them.	*I know I haven't given you much attention today. After I change my clothes and make one quick call, let's play a game together.*

NEW MESSAGE	*HOW I WANT TO RESPOND*

TRIGGERS, MESSAGES AND RESPONSES TO MY CHILDREN'S BEHAVIOR THIS WEEK AS WELL AS MY NEW MESSAGES AND THE RESPONSES I WANT TO HAVE TO MY CHILDREN'S NEEDS.

DAY	*TRIGGER*	*MESSAGE I GAVE MYSELF*

RESPONSE	*NEW MESSAGE*	*DESIRED RESPONSE*

DAY	TRIGGER	MESSAGE I GAVE MYSELF

RESPONSE	NEW MESSAGE	DESIRED RESPONSE

While we are actively trying to change the messages we are teaching our children about anger expression, it is often helpful to really listen to what our children are telling us in their words and behavior. Older children and youth can frequently tell us what makes them angry. Sometimes they can tell us what they do when they're angry, and sometimes we can let them know what we observe in their behavior.

PICK A TIME IN THE NEXT FEW WEEKS AND ASK YOUR OLDER CHILDREN WHAT KINDS OF THINGS MAKE THEM ANGRY. (Because a great deal of anger can be generated toward the behaviors of those closest to them, don't be surprised if some of their anger is at your behavior. Even though you may want to be defensive, keep reminding yourself that their feedback is a gift.)

Below are examples of the things children have told me that make them angry and what they do with their anger.

Example:

WHAT MAKES ME ANGRY?	WHAT I DO WITH MY ANGER
I get angry when my mom and dad fight.	I go to my room and shut the door.
I get angry when adults say one thing and do another.	I stop listening. I start a fight.
I get angry when my brother goes into my room without asking.	I hit him.
I get angry when adults ruin the environment.	Nothing.
I get angry when my parents work all the time.	Try to get their attention, then they get mad.
I get angry when people break promises.	Get depressed.

WHAT MAKES MY CHILDREN ANGRY?   WHAT DO THEY DO?

DESENSITIZATION
AND
OPERANT CONDITIONING

In his book *On Killing: The Psychological Cost of Learning to Kill in War and Society* (1995, pp. 3–4, 30, 35), Lt. Col. David Grossman presents the results of research conducted by G. Dyer, R. Gabriel and S. L. A. Marshall asserting that the vast majority of soldiers in both world wars never fired a shot. Most fighter pilots, furthermore, never shot anyone down or even tried to. Grossman contends that even though many people ignored the research of individuals like Marshall, the U.S. Army did not. They changed training procedures for the military, with the result that 55 percent of soldiers in Korea fired their weapons. Still other advanced techniques, spurred by greater developments in technology and psychology, resulted in 90 to 95 percent of our soldiers being willing to kill in Vietnam.

The techniques that were so successful in training the military in Vietnam—progressive desensitization and operant conditioning—are now increasingly offered to the general population. Desensitization techniques used to train soldiers in Vietnam involved increasing exposure to films that showed explicit and brutal footage of people being violently injured and killed. The senseless and brutal violence shown to soldiers in the military to teach them to kill is frighteningly similar to the images currently available to our youth in movie theaters, on television and in video games.

Many of the young people who commit acts of violence spend hours in front of the television set watching violence and hours shooting guns in the video arcades. Watching television alone, the average child sees two hundred thousand violent acts by high school graduation. This does not count the violence witnessed in movie theaters, video arcades, or in their homes and community. Our nation's children cheer when the blood spurts out of their victims in video games or when the victor rips out the spinal cord of the opponent. Our children listen to music that refers to women as "bitches" and "whores."

THE GREATEST ANTIDOTE FOR THE UNHEALTHY ANGER EXPRESSED BY OUR CHILDREN IS OUR AWARENESS. FROM YOUR MEMORY ALONE, ANSWER THE FOLLOWING QUESTIONS.

How many hours of television does your child watch during the week?

What are the television shows your child watches weekly?

What are the video games your child plays?

What is the music your child listens to?

What were the last ten movies your child watched in the movie theater or on home video?

Listen to the evening news one night and record every violent message you hear:

SELECT A WEEK IN THE NEAR FUTURE WHEN YOU CAN SPEND EVENINGS AND WEEKENDS WITH YOUR CHILDREN. PLAY THE GAMES THEY PLAY ON THE COMPUTER OR IN THE VIDEO ARCADE. ASK THEM TO WATCH THE LAST FIVE MOVIES THEY WATCHED WITH YOU. WATCH THE TELEVISION PROGRAMS THEY WATCH WITH THEM. ASK THEM TO SHARE THE MUSIC THEY LISTEN TO. IF YOU HAVE DIFFICULTY UNDER-STANDING THE WORDS, ASK THEM TO TELL YOU WHAT THEY ARE OR READ THE LYRICS ON THE FOLDOUT INSIDE THE COVER IF THEY ARE AVAILABLE. RECORD THE VIOLENT MESSAGES YOU SAW AND HEARD DURING THE WEEK AND THE MESSAGES ABOUT ANGER THAT YOUR CHILD IS BEING TAUGHT.

Violent Messages I Heard/Saw on Television:

Violent Messages I Heard/Saw in the Movies:

Violent Messages I Heard/Saw While Playing the Video Games:

Violent Messages I Heard from the Songs My Child/Youth Listens to:

What I Have Learned That My Child/Youth Is Being Taught About Anger Expression in the Movies, on Television, in Music and Through Video Games:

Plans for Limiting My Child/Youth's Exposure to Violence:

Example:

I will limit their television viewing.

I will watch shows with him or her and discuss them.

I will only allow video games that are teaching tools and are nonviolent.

FAMILY VALUES

Rather than learning values that support connectedness and interconnectedness, many children learn values that support violence. Children are not born with a concept of self, but develop it over the first eight years of life. Children take from the outside and bring to the inside the concept of who they are as they learn about themselves, from adult role models, other people and life. This teaching comes from their environment, what is mirrored back to them through role models and experiences.

The way a child learns respect is to be respected and to watch adult role models treat themselves, others and all of creation with respect. I talked to a mother in a grocery store recently who had just hit her child for hitting his brother. This child is not learning to use words and not strike out, but learns instead that you can hit if you're bigger.

Children who lack consistent models frequently search for them in their extended family or the broader community: a teacher, policeman, spiritual leader, etc. If they don't find them at home or in the community, they will find them instead in rock stars or Hollywood antiheroes. These unhealthy role models have increasing influence on the lives of our young people.

Celebrities also provide solace for many adults who aren't connected enough to come to know their next-door neighbor. They focus a tremendous amount of energy keeping up with the lives of actors and actresses, talk-show hosts, sports heroes, royalty and other celebrities. People may not sit down for a family dinner, listening to their children share stories of their day and offering their own, but instead relax eating alone while watching sports or a celebrity gossip show, or poring over a magazine.

Many of us feel a sense of isolation and disconnection from those around us. We spend our free time watching television and movies, reading magazines, and developing heroes and models far away; or we buy things that only temporarily fill an empty space. It might be useful for us and for the emotional health of future generations and society to occasionally turn around and look into the faces of the children who are following us.

I heard a father cautioning his child, "You can't let yourself be stepped on. You've got to look out for Number One. If you have to step on a few people on the way, so be it." Another parent might tell a child to care for others and share, and yet cuts in front of everyone in the grocery line. The message which is taught is the one that is seen, not the one that is heard.

Many youths have told me the values they are learning in their families and communities, often ones that can lead to competition and violence rather than connection and cooperation. Check your own way of life against this list as well as considering the actions of society at large. It is helpful to sit down with your family and take the time to go over the list. Add to the list. Remember, these are not only the values taught in the home, but in magazines, advertisements and in the community as a whole:

____ Always tell others that I'm just fine.

____ I need it now! Gratification has to happen immediately. Who wants to save? Buy on credit.

____ Might is right.

____ Don't get involved.

____ It's important to beat out the other guy before he gets ahead of you.

____ Get ahead any way you can.

____ Women are objects.

____ Men don't feel.

____ My beliefs are right and yours are wrong.

____ Violence is an appropriate way to handle disagreement.

____ Money is more important than relationships.

____ Talk about people, not to people.

____ I'm not accountable unless I get caught.

____ Blame others for your problems.

____ It's not all right to have emotional needs. Take a pill, be happy.

____ I can only be heard if I talk louder or show you who's boss.

____ Childhood is overrated. Grow up fast so I can get on with my life.

____ You can get anything you want if you have enough money.

____ Look out for Number One!

____ Hurry up! Hurry up!

____ Those are your kids, not mine.

____

____

____

____

____

____

———
———
———
———
———
———
———

NOW THINK OF THE VALUES THAT YOU WANT TO HAVE AS THE FOUN-
DATION OF YOUR FAMILY. TOGETHER, MAKE A LIST OF THOSE VALUES. I
HAVE LISTED FOUR VALUES AS EXAMPLES:

___ Healthy family relationships are a priority.
___ Cooperation.
___ It is all right to have differences of opinion.
___ We are responsible and accountable for our actions.
———
———
———
———
———
———
———
———
———
———
———
———
———
———
———

LIST THE BEHAVIORS IN YOUR FAMILY THAT SUPPORT THE VALUES YOU WANT AS THE FOUNDATION FOR YOUR LIFE AND THOSE THAT UNDERMINE THEM. MAKE AN ACTION PLAN THAT WILL SUPPORT THE VALUES YOU HAVE CHOSEN:

Example:

CURRENT BEHAVIORS THAT SUPPORT OUR CHOSEN VALUES	*BEHAVIORS THAT UNDERMINE THE VALUES WE WANT TO LIVE BY*
We always spend Sundays together. *We have fun summer vacations.*	*We rarely eat meals together.* *We spend most weekends catching up on chores. We rarely have time set aside just for fun.*

CURRENT BEHAVIORS THAT SUPPORT OUR CHOSEN VALUES

BEHAVIORS THAT UNDERMINE THE VALUES WE WANT TO LIVE BY

ACTION PLANS FOR CHANGE:

Example:

We will eat dinner together at least four times a week.

We will take the time once a week for a fun family activity chosen by the whole family.

Many children are being diagnosed with attention deficit disorder (ADD). This in some children has its underpinnings in excessive exposure to out-of-control, technology-based "entertainment"; lack of protein in the morning; learning styles that conflict with the way the child is being taught; or stresses at home. If your child has been diagnosed with ADD or ADHD, it is important that adult caretakers limit television time, restrict video games, make sure that the child eats some protein in the morning, make certain the child has plenty of fresh air and exercise, are aware of stresses in the child's life, and know the child's learning style. Even if your child is not hyperactive, it is important to ensure your child's continued health. Change begins with awareness.

The number of hours our (my) child watches television on an average day? _____

The number of hours our (my) child plays video games on an average day? _____

The foods our (my) child ate for breakfast last week:

Sunday:

Monday:

Tuesday:

Wednesday:

Thursday:

Friday:

Saturday:

How many hours does our (my) child exercise on an average day?_____

Our (my) child's learning style:

> Example:
>
> *Our child learns by doing. He has difficulty reading.*

The current stresses in our (my) child's life:

> Example:
>
> *Our child witnessed my partner shoving me last week.*
>
> *My wife and I recently divorced.*
>
> *Her grandma died a couple of months ago.*

Think of some changes you might make that would promote the health of your child. Develop action plans below.

> Example:
>
> *I (we) am going to stop giving my child sugary cereal in the morning and will offer yogurt instead.*
>
> *I (we) am going to enroll my child in the martial arts class that has been advertised.*
>
> *My (our) child has had difficulty reading. I am going to ask for help to determine his learning style and advocate for him being taught in the way he learns.*
>
> *I (we) am going to talk to our child about her grandmother's death. I haven't talked to her about it before.*

ACTION PLANS TO ENSURE THE HEALTH OF OUR (MY) CHILD(REN):

ACTION PLANS TO ENSURE THE HEALTH OF OUR (MY) CHILD(REN):

Many parents, grandparents, aunts, uncles, teachers and community members are concerned about the violence potential in their children. Below are some warning signs that might signal causes for concern:

Social withdrawal
Excessive mood changes
Feelings of rejection
Feelings of unworthiness
Feelings of isolation
Bullying behavior
Poor academic performance
Intolerance for differences
Discipline problems
Aggressive behavior
Drawings, stories or poetry of aggression directed at a specific person or group
Skipping school
Shoplifting
Difficulty eating or sleeping
Uncontrollable anger
Impulsive behaviors
Threats of violence
Use of drugs or alcohol
Aggression toward animals
Gang activities
Preoccupation with weapons
Preoccupation with violence

If a child shows the warning signs listed above, offer support to the child and his or her family. Seek out the support of counselors, teachers, extended family, coaches, peers, spiritual leaders who are connected with the family and community members who may have or might develop a caring relationship with the child.

SECTION ELEVEN

REBUILDING COMMUNITIES

Many Native American and First Nations elders refer to a time when people knew the importance of "standing each other up" or "staking each other down," which simply means standing together, never letting anyone stand alone. In the circle of community we are all relatives, members of the human race, working side by side and needing support from one another. Yet, over the decades, the circle has slowly broken down and reformed into a pyramid, disconnecting and disempowering us. A child being abused in public is often ignored, and the screams of many elderly go unheard.

A long time ago coal miners practiced a certain survival custom. They would always take a canary with them into the mines. If the canary became ill and began to die, the miners would know that a toxic, odorless gas had seeped into the mine and would eventually cause a decrease in the oxygen supply. If we take the time to listen to children and youth, and really see what is happening today, we will be immediately aware that our children have become the canaries in our community.

One afternoon I was having a discussion with my late husband, who had grown up in a major metropolitan area and had worked early in his career as a counselor with violent gangs in New York City. I had grown up in the country and was interested in his thoughts about the changing sense of community in large urban areas. He said, "Things changed a lot when housing projects were built and people left their front stoops. Among other things, crime began to steadily increase."

I learned that sociologists actually had a name for this aspect of life in large cities:

"Front Stoop Neighborhood Control." In the fifties and earlier, family life in cities used to encompass sitting out on the front stoops of apartment buildings and small houses during all hours of the day and evening. Families socialized and swapped stories about the old country, earlier days, and the difficulties of city life, or shared the most current information about children or families. They also kept an eye on the neighborhood children and were acutely aware of the comings and goings of people on their block. When the huge new building projects were constructed after World War II, front stoops became less common, and a very important and necessary aspect of community life in the cities disappeared.

Suburban homeowners built fences, both literally and figuratively. Neighbors began fencing themselves in and adjoining families out. Fences and other obstructions to communication became more imposing over the years as fear in community life increased. People began demanding more privacy. Isolation increased and conversation decreased. Arguments between neighbors began to flourish over whose dog was on whose lawn, who should paint and repair the fence, whose children were running through the yards, who was acceptable in the neighborhood or who was going to sue whom over what.

Richard Louv, in his disquieting book *Childhood's Future*, speaks about the supportive network that every child needs in order to grow into a healthy adult. He calls this network a web. "The web is emotional as well as physical. As a boy growing up in a troubled family, I sensed that I could get much of what I needed from the web—neighbors to watch out for me on the street, schools that cared, and an understandable community in which to prove myself. . . . Once the web begins to unravel, the smallest bodies fall through first." (1990, p. 6)

TAKE SOME TIME AND EXPLORE YOUR "WEB." WHO ARE YOUR NEIGHBORS? DO YOU KNOW THEIR CHILDREN? DO THEY KNOW YOURS? WHO ARE THE NEIGHBORS (single mothers, working families, recent widows, those that are physically challenged) THAT CAN USE SOME ASSISTANCE? WHAT ASSISTANCE COULD YOU ASK FOR?

MY NEIGHBORS ARE:

MY NEIGHBORS WHO MIGHT NEED ASSISTANCE:

> Example:
>
> *Mrs. Jones has been recently widowed. She is retired and knows few people in the neighborhood. Her children and grandchildren live many miles away.*

HOW I MIGHT ASSIST MY NEIGHBORS:

> Example:
>
> *I could invite Mrs. Jones to join us for dinner once a week.*
>
> *Mr. Smith is developmentally challenged. I could offer to pick up things he might need at the store when I go.*

ASSISTANCE THAT I MIGHT NEED FROM MY NEIGHBORS:

Example:

I am at work most days and sometimes I travel. It would be helpful to know that someone is keeping an eye on my house. I've been robbed once.

I am a single mother, and sometimes it would be helpful to know there is someone there when I am overextended or in times of emergency.

WHO I MIGHT ASK FOR ASSISTANCE:

Example:

Mr. Smith lives right next door and often sits by his window. I might ask him if he would be willing to pay attention to my house when I gone. I'll have to trim my bushes a bit so he can see activity around my house.

Mrs. Jones has raised many children and loves children. I could ask her to be an adopted grandma to my children. My mom died last year and I miss her. My dad lives with my brother seven hours away.

I SPOKE TO MY NEIGHBORS ABOUT MY NEEDS AS WELL AS OFFERING THEM ASSISTANCE. THIS IS WHAT I LEARNED:

Example:

Mr. Smith said he would love it if I could check with him when I went to the store. He said he would be happy to keep an eye on my house. He told me he does anyway, but it has been hard to see clearly with my bushes in the way.

Mrs. Jones cried when I asked her to be a kind of adopted grandma to my children. She said she was honored and would love to join us for a meal. She also said that she would be glad to have Susie and Mark over to play games or do some art. She's a retired schoolteacher. She misses her children and grandchildren.

WHAT I LEARNED FROM MY NEIGHBORS (continued):

Many people are beginning efforts to take back their communities and strengthen the connections that allow them to be healthy: mentally, emotionally, spiritually and physically. In a peaceful community in Washington state, a hate group attempted to drive out and intimidate people of color. However, people stood together and made it clear there was no room in their community for hate.

In a small New England community, people came together to support small businesses that they felt were far more than businesses. "They are a way of life that is fast disappearing. When I needed help, it was the local grocer that offered me temporary assistance. My children feel at home in that family-run store."

In another community, a veteran of the Vietnam War was invited to guide the community through an ancient ceremony from his culture that welcomed home those who had been to war. The men and women stood together, veterans of World War II, Korea, Vietnam and the Gulf War. Tears that had never been cried streamed down the faces as the veterans held each other up, as one community member after another came up to welcome them home. One man said, "I never realized how much we needed each other. She has lived right next door for years and years, and I had no idea how much pain she carried from Korea. I don't think I even knew she had been in the armed services. We could have supported one another. I was there, too."

Television shows like *Picket Fences* and *Northern Exposure* soared to the top of the ratings because most of us are drawn to the idea of community: the local judge modeling values and wisdom; the general practice doctor who knows the family; the local grocer who is willing to run a tab; and community members of all professions and backgrounds struggling together on behalf of their children, the elderly, and each other. These are the images we cherish.

THINK OF SOME THINGS YOUR COMMUNITY COULD DO TO STRENGTHEN THE WEB. WHO COULD YOU CONTACT TO HELP MAKE YOUR IDEAS A REALITY?

Example:

We don't know each other's children in the neighborhood. Maybe we could have a picnic in the park to welcome the children. It would let them know how much they mean to all of us.

WHO COULD I REACH OUT TO THAT MIGHT SUPPORT MY IDEA:

Examples:

Mrs. Jones, Mr. Smith, the teachers at the school . . .

Many of us learned throughout the 1950s and 1960s that a movement must have a vision. In order to move the present toward a healthy future, we must not only know what we are against, but also what we support. Too often people expend a great deal of energy complaining about relationships, the way others treat them, politics, the state of health care, etc. I usually ask, "What ideas do you have that you believe will make a difference? How much time and energy are you willing to commit to actualize your vision? How can I help?"

If our imaginations are limited to continued illness, unhappy relationships, depression, building more jails, isolation and degradation, we shouldn't be surprised when we live what we imagine. Too often, we blame others, expecting them to change things for us. Then we complain about the actions that were taken and feel angry when things stay the same.

By creating a vision of how we want our personal lives to be and then branching out to how we want our communities and society to act, we begin to move toward the positive goals of emotional health in all areas of our lives. When we achieve that health, we'll find ourselves in balance.

MY VISION FOR MYSELF AND MY FAMILY:

AFTER REVIEWING THE WORK YOU HAVE COMPLETED IN THE WORKBOOK, LIST THE STEPS YOU CAN TAKE TO MAKE YOUR PERSONAL VISION A REALITY:

MY VISION FOR MY COMMUNITY:

THE VISIONS OF AT LEAST TWO OF MY NEIGHBORS:

OUR COMBINED VISION:

WHAT EACH OF US CAN DO TO MAKE OUR VISION A REALITY:

THE GHOSTS THAT MIGHT KEEP ME STUCK:

Example:

Nobody cares.

What can we do? We don't have any power.

People are dangerous.

MESSAGES I CAN USE TO COMMUNICATE WITH THE GHOSTS THAT KEEP ME FROM WORKING TOWARD REBUILDING MY COMMUNITY:

Example:

Of course people care. Consider all the people who volunteer in times of disaster. We all want to do something. We have learned to feel helpless.

We have a great deal of power as a community. Most things that have changed in this world have changed because of community people taking a stand, not merely through government programs.

Yes, some people are at risk and have hurt others. Many more people are supportive. We need to come together in order to intervene with people at risk to do harm. Many would make changes in their lives with the support of others. We can be instrumental in guiding them toward help. If we concentrate on the person as well as the behavior, change can happen. That's what community is all about. The danger comes when we isolate, become apathetic and don't stand together.

MESSAGES I CAN USE TO COMMUNICATE WITH THE GHOSTS THAT KEEP ME FROM WORKING TOWARD HEALTHY CHANGE IN MY COMMUNITY.

BIBLIOGRAPHY

BOOKS

Abdullah, Sharif M. *The Power of One: Authentic Leadership in Turbulent Times.* Philadelphia: New Society Publishers, 1995.

Akbar, Na'im. *Chains and Images of Psychological Slavery.* Jersey City, New Jersey: New Mind Productions, 1984.

Allcorn, Seth. *Anger in the Workplace: Understanding Aggression and Violence.* Wesport, Ct.: Quorum Books, 1994.

Anonymous. "The Companions of Duty." In *Changing Community (The Graywolf Annual 10).* Scott Walker (Ed.). St. Paul, Minn.: Grey Wolf Press, 1993: 135.

Arrien, Angeles. *The Four-Fold Way: Walking the Paths of the Warrior, Teacher, Healer & Visionary.* San Francisco: HarperCollins, 1993.

Bettelheim, Bruno. *Surviving and Other Essays.* New York: Vintage Books, 1980.

Bowlby, John. *Attachment and Loss: Volume III, Loss, Sadness and Depression.* New York: Basic Books, Inc., 1980.

Bramson, Robert M. *Coping with Difficult People.* New York: Doubleday, Anchor Books, 1981.

Cannon, Walter. *Bodily Changes in Pain: Hunger, Fear and Rage.* New York: Appleton, 1929.

Cousins, Norman. *Anatomy of an Illness.* New York: W. W. Norton and Company, 1979.

Cox, T. "Stress: A Psychophysiological Approach to Cancer." In *Psychosocial Stress and Cancer.* C. L. Cooper (Ed.). New York: John Wiley, 1984: 149–169.

Davis, Angela Yvonne. *Angela Davis: An Autobiography.* New York: International Publishing, 1989.

Derber, Charles. *The Wilding of America: How Greed and Violence are Eroding Our Nation's Character.* New York: St. Martin's Press, 1996.

Dershowitz, Alan M. *The Abuse Excuse: And Other Cop-Outs, Sob Stories, Evasions of Responsibility.* New York: Little, Brown and Company, Backbay Books, 1994.

Dyer, G. *War.* London, England: Guild Publishing, 1985.

Esler, Gavin. *United States of Anger: The People and the American Dream.* New York: Michael Joseph Limited, Penguin Books USA, Inc., 1997.

Ewing, Charles Patrick. *Kids Who Kill.* Lexington, Ky.: Lexington Books, 1990.

Eyre, Linda, and Richard Eyre. *Life Balance: How to Simplify and Bring Harmony to Your Everyday Life.* New York: Simon & Schuster, Fireside, 1997.

Freire, Paulo. *Pedagogy of the Oppressed.* New Revised 20th Anniversary Edition, Translated by Myra Bergman Ramos. New York: Continuum, 1993.

Friedman, Meyer, and Ray Rosenman. *Type A Behavior and Your Heart.* New York: Knopf, 1974.

Gabriel, R. A. *Military Psychiatry: A Comparative Perspective.* New York: Greenport Press, 1986.

Gilligan, James. *Violence: Reflections on a National Epidemic.* New York: Random House, Vintage Books, 1997.

Glasser, William. *Choice Theory: A New Psychology of Personal Freedom.* New York: HarperCollins, 1998.

Grossman, David. *On Killing, The Psychological Cost of Learning to Kill in War and Society.* Boston: Little, Brown, and Company, 1995.

Groth, A. Nicholas, with H. Jean Birnbaum. *Men Who Rape: The Psychology of the Offender.* New York: Plenum Press, 1979.

Haynal, Andre, Miklos Molnar, and Gerard De Puymege. *Fanaticism: A Historical and Psychoanalytical Study.* New York: Schocken Books, 1983.

Huxley, Aldous. *Brave New World.* New York: Bantam, Harper and Brothers, 1939.

Irwin, J., and H. Anisman. "Stress and Pathology: Immunological and Central Nervous System Interactions." In *Psychological Stress and Cancer.* C. L. Cooper (Ed.). New York: John Wiley, 1984.

Jacobson, Neil, and John Gottman. *When Men Batter Women: New Insights into Ending Abusive Relationships.* New York: Simon & Schuster, 1998.

Jamison, Kaleel. *The Nibble Theory and the Kernel of Power. A Book About Leadership, Self-Empowerment, and Personal Growth.* Mahwah, N.J.: Paulist Press, 1984.

Jensen, Jean C. *Reclaiming Your Life: A Step-by-Step Guide to Using Regression Therapy to Overcome the Effects of Childhood Abuse.* Hammondsworth, Middlesex, England: Dutton, 1995.

Kang, H. S. *Dong Yang Euitiak Gaeron (Introduction to East Asian Medicine).* Seoul: Komun-sa, 1981.

Lamb, Sharon. *The Trouble with Blame: Victims, Perpetrators and Responsibility.* Cambridge, Mass.: Harvard University Press, 1996.

Lawrence, Marilyn, ed. *Fed Up and Hungry: Women, Oppression and Food.* New York: Peter Bedrick Books, 1987.

Lee, S. H. *In This Earth and That Wind: This Is Korea.* D. I. Steinberg (Trans.). Seoul: Hollym. Corp., 1967.

Lefkowitz, Bernard. *Our Guys.* New York: Random House, Vintage Books, 1997.

Leo, John. "Community and Personal Duty." In *Changing Community (The Graywolf Annual 10).* Scott Walker (Ed.). St. Paul, Minn. Grey Wolf Press, 1993: 29–32.

Lerner, Harriet Goldhor. *The Dance of Intimacy.* New York: Harper and Row, 1989.

Lerner, Michael. *Surplus Powerlessness.* Oakland, Calif.: The Institute for Labor and Mental Health, 1986.

Lewis, Dorothy Otnow. *Guilty by Reason of Insanity: A Psychiatrist Explores the Minds of Killers.* New York: Random House, Ballantine Books, 1998.

Louv, Richard. *Childhood's Future.* New York: Anchor Books, 1990.

Lorenz, Konrad. *On Aggression.* London, England: Methuen and Company, 1967.

Marshall, S. L. A. *Men Against Fire.* Gloucester, Mass.: Peter Smith, 1978.

McKay, Matthew, Peter Rogers, and Judith McKay. *When Anger Hurts: Quieting the Storm Within.* Oakland, Calif.: New Harbinger Publications, 1989.

McKay, Matthew, Patrick Fanning, Kim Paleg, and Dana Landis. *When Anger Hurts Your Kids: A Parent's Guide.* New York: MJF Books, 1996.

Medina, John. *Depression: How It Happens, How It's Healed.* Oakland, Calif.: CME, Inc., New Harbinger, 1998.

Middelton-Moz, Jane. *Children of Trauma: Rediscovering Your Discarded Self.* Deerfield Beach, Fla.: Health Communications, Inc., 1989.

———. *Shame and Guilt: Master of Disguise.* Deerfield Beach, Fla.: Health Communications, Inc., 1990.

———. *Will to Survive: Affirming the Positive Power of the Human Spirit.* Deerfield Beach, Fla.: Health Communications, Inc., 1992.

Middelton-Moz, Jane, and Lorie Dwinell. *After the Tears: Reclaiming the Personal Losses of Childhood.* Deerfield Beach, Fla.: Health Communications, Inc., 1986.

Miller, Alice. *The Untouched Key, Tracing Childhood Trauma in Creativity and Destructiveness.* New York: Doubleday, 1988.

Mills, Nicholaus. *The Triumph of Meanness: America's War Against Its Better Self.* Reading, Mass.: Houghton-Mifflin Company, 1997.

Nuckols, Cardwell C., and Bill Chickering. *Healing an Angry Heart: Finding Solace in a Hostile World.* Deerfield Beach, Fla.: Health Communications, 1998.

Ochberg, Frank M. *Post-Traumatic Therapy and Victims of Violence.* New York: Brunner/Mazel, 1988.

Papolos, Demitri, and Janice Papolos. *Overcoming Depression. (3rd ed.)* New York: HarperCollins, 1996.

Pipher, Mary. *The Shelter of Each Other: Rebuilding Our Families.* New York: Ballantine Books, 1996.

Potter-Efron, Ronald. *Angry All the Time: An Emergency Guide to Anger Control.* Oakland, Calif.: New Harbinger Publications, 1994.

Potter-Efron, Ronald, and Patricia Potter-Efron. *Anger, Alcoholism, and Addiction: Treating Individuals, Couples, and Families.* New York: W. W. Norton and Company, 1991.

———. *Letting Go of Anger: The Ten Most Common Anger Styles and What To Do About Them.* Oakland, Calif.: New Harbinger Publications, 1995.

Real, Terrence. *I Don't Want To Talk About It: Overcoming the Secret Legacy of Male Depression.* New York: Simon & Schuster, Fireside, 1997.

Robson, Ruthann. "Marbalo Lesbian Separatism and Neutering Male Cats." In Jess Wells, *Lesbians Raising Sons.* Los Angeles, New York: Alyson Books, 1997.

Roy, Maria, ed. *The Abusive Partner.* New York: Von Nostrand Reinhold Company, 1982.

Rubin, Theodore Isaac. *The Angry Book.* Toronto: The Macmillan Company, 1969.

———. *Compassion and Self-Hate: An Alternative to Despair.* New York: Simon & Schuster, Touchstone, 1998.

Schlessinger, Dr. Laura. *How Could You Do That?! The Abdication of Character, Courage, and Conscience.* New York: HarperPerennial, 1996.

Seligman, Martin E. P. *Helplessness: On Depression, Development, and Death.* New York: W. H. Freeman and Company, 1975.

Seltzer, Mark. *Serial Killers: Death and Life in America's Wounded Culture.* New York: Routledge, 1998.

Shulman, Bernard H. *Contributions to Individual Psychology.* Chicago: Alfred Adler Institute of Chicago, 1973.

Tannen, Deborah. *The Argument Culture: Moving from Debate to Dialogue.* New York: Random House, 1998.

Tavris, Carol. *Anger: The Misunderstood Emotion.* New York: Simon & Schuster, Touchstone, 1982, revised 1989.

Thomas, Sandra, and Cheryl Jefferson. *Use Your Anger: A Woman's Guide to Empowerment.* New York: Simon & Schusterr, Pocket Books, 1996.

Wattenberg, Ben J. *Values Matter Most: How Republicans or Democrats or a Third Party Can Win and Renew the American Way of Life.* New York: Simon & Schuster, The Free Press, 1995.

Wells, Jess, ed. *Lesbians Raising Sons.* Los Angeles: Alyson Publications, 1997.

Williams, Redford, and Virginia Williams. *Anger Kills: Seventeen Strategies for Controlling the Hostility That Can Harm Your Health.* New York: HarperCollins, 1993.

PERIODICALS

Baer, P. E., F. H. Collins, G.C. Bouriano, and M. F. Ketchel. *"Assessing Personality Factors in Essential Hypertension with a Brief Self-Report Instrument."* Psychosomatic Medicine 7 (1969): pp. 653–659.

Baker, Donald P. "As Kentucky Town Mourns, Movie Suggested as Basis for Boy's Attack." *Washington Post.* December 6, 1997: page A3.

Barefoot, J. C., W. G. Dahlstrom, and R. D. Williams Jr. "Hostility, CHD Incidence, and Total Mortality: A 25-Year Follow-up Study of 255 Physicians." *Psychosomatic Medicine* 45 (1983): pp. 59–63.

Beck, Melinda. "Voices: Food Banks and Marriage Counseling; Marchers Home with Plans to Make a Difference. On America Online, February 4, 1997.

Connell, Dominic, Matthew Joint, and Louis Mizell. "Aggressive Driving: Three Studies," AAA Foundation for Traffic Safety, March 1997.

Cowley, Geoffrey. "Why Children Turn Violent." *Newsweek.* April 6, 1998: pp. 23–26.

Fox, B. H. "The Role of Psychological Factors in Cancer Incidence and Prognosis." *Oncology* 9/3 (1995): pp. 245–253.

Gegax, Trent, Jerry Adler, and Daniel Pedersen. "The Schoolyard Killers: Behind the Ambush." *Newsweek,* April 6, 1998: pp. 19–24.

Grosch, William N. "Shame, Rage and Addiction." *Psychiatric Quarterly* 65/1 (1994): pp. 49–63.

Harburg, E., E. H. Blakelock, and P. J. Roper. "Resentful and Reflective Coping with Arbitrary Authority and Blood Pressure: Detroit." *Psychosomatic Medicine* 41 (1979): pp. 189–202.

Hunt, Steven, and Gina Delmastro. "The Body Cries." *Focus on Family* July/August 1985.

Jensen, R., and J. Shaw "Children as Victims of War: Current Knowledge and Futher Research Needs." *Journal of the American Academy Child Adolescent Psychiatry* 4 (1993): pp. 697–708.

Kaplan, S., L. A. Go, H. S. Chalk, E. Magliocco, D. Rohouit, and W. Ross. "Hostility in Verbal Productions and Hypnotic Dreams in Hypertensive Patients." *Psychosomatic Medicine* 23 (1961): pp. 311–322.

Kaye, Ken. "Airline Seeks Ways to Ground Sky Rage." *Sun-Sentinel,* August 31, 1998.

Kesey, Ken. "Land of the Free, Home of the Bullets." *Rolling Stone.* July 9–23, 1998: pp. 51–56.

Kune, Gabriel, Susan Kune, Lyndsey Watson, and Claus Bahnson. "Personalitiy as a Risk Factor in Large Bowel Cancer: Data from the Melbourne Colorectal Cancer Study." *Psychological Medicine* 21/1 (1991): pp. 29–41.

Mann, A. H. "Psychiatric Morbidity and Hostility in Hypertension," *Psychological Medicine* 7 (1977): pp. 653–659.

Matshe, Thoko, "The Myths of Rape," Vol. 2. Woman Plus, 9–01–1997, pp. 3–4, Infonautics Corporation, 1998.

McGaha, Johnny. "Alcoholism and the Chemically Dependent Family: A Study of Adult Felons on Probation." *Journal of Offender Rehabilitation.* 193–4 (1993): pp. 57–69.

Morris, T. and S. Greer. "Psychological Atributes of Women Who Develop Breast Cancer: A Controlled Study." *Journal of Psychosomatic Research* 19 (1975): pp. 147–153.

Morrow, Lance. "Behavior Unspeakable." *Time*, (Feb. 22, 1993): p. 48

Munhall, Patricia. "Women's Anger: A Phenomenological Perspective." *Health Care for Women International* 14/6 (1993): pp. 481–491.

Northam, Sarah, and Stephen D. Bluen. "Differential Correlates of Components of Type A Behavior." *South African Journal of Psychology* 24/3 (1994): pp. 131–137.

Palfai, Tibor P., and Kenneth Hart. "Anger Coping Styles and Perceived Social Support." *Journal of Social Psychology* 137/ 4 (1997): pp. 405–411.

Pang, Keum Young. "Hwabyung: The Construction of a Korean Popular Illness Among Korean Elderly Immigrant Women in the United States." *Culture, Medicine and Psychiatry* 144 (Dec. 1990): pp. 495–512.

"Petition Drive Seeks Charges Against Killer's Friend." *The Las Vegas Sun*, August 22, 1998.

Rado, S. "The Problem of Melancholia." *The International Journal of Analysis* 9 (1928): pp. 420–438.

Richters, J. E., and R. Martinez. "The NIMH Community Violence Project 1: Children as Victims of and Witnesses to Violence." *Psychiatry* 56 (1993): pp. 7–21.

Schacter, J. "Pain, Fear and Anger in Hypertensives and Normotensives." *Psychosomatic Medicine* 19 (1957): pp. 17–29.

Scheir, M. F. and M. W. Bridges. "Person Variables and Health: Personality Predispositions and Acute Psychological States as Shared Determinants for Disease" (Review). *Psychosomatic Medicine* 57/3 (1995): pp. 255–268.

Swanson, Janice, Suzanne Dibble, and Carole Chenitz. "Clinical Features and Psychosocial Factors in Young Adults with Genital Herpes." *Image: The Journal of Nursing Scholarships* 27/1 (1995): pp. 16–22.

Talan, Jamie. "Sick or Stressed Out?" *Psychology Today* (July/August 1998): p. 18.

———. "Cardiac Consciousness-Raising." *Psychology Today* (July/August 1998): p. 18.

Temoshock, L., B. W. Heller, and R. W. Sagebriel. "The Relationship of Psychosocial Factors to Prognostic Indicators in Cutaneous Malignant Melanoma." *Journal of Psychosomatic Research* 29 (1985): pp. 135–153.

Thomas, Sandra P. "Relationships of Suppression to Blood Pressure. International Congress of Behavioral Medicine, Washington, District of Columbia, US." *Nursing Research* 466 (Nov.–Dec. 1997): pp. 324–330.

Wagner, Angie. "Casino Slaying Case Set for Trial." The Associated Press AP–NY–08–29–98, 1309 EDT.

Watson, Maggie, Steven Greer, Linda Rowden, Christine Gorman, et al. "Relationships Between Emotional Control, Adjustment to Cancer and Depression and Anxiety in Breast Cancer Patients." *Psychological Medicine* 21/1 (1991): pp. 51–57.

Williams, Redford B., et al. "Psychosocial Correlates of Job Strain in a Sample of Working Women." *Archives of General Psychiatry* 54 (1997): pp. 543–548.

NOTES

Other Books by Jane Middelton-Moz

Welcoming Our Children to a New Millennium

Children and adults express their thoughts and wishes for the new era in this heartwarming daybook, a celebration of youth, families, communities and our future.

Code #7427 • Quality Paperback • $12.95

Children of Trauma

Learn how unresolved childhood trauma can reverberate through generations. This book will help you find and heal your discarded self.

Code #0147 • Quality Paperback • $9.95

Shame and Guilt

An insightful masterpiece that will take you by the hand and lead you on a journey toward self-love and self-acceptance.

Code #0724 • Quality Paperback • $8.95

BOOKS FOR BETTER LIVING
AND PEACE OF MIND

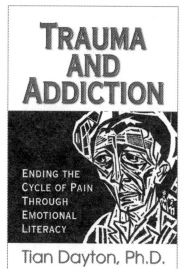

Trauma and Addiction
By Tian Dayton

This fascinating book identifies the inter-connection of trauma and addictive behavior, and shows why they can become an unending cycle. It offers effective ways to work through our traumas in order to heal our addictions, be they to substances, activities and/or possessions. For anyone caught in the destructive cycle of trauma and addiction or for those treating the symptoms, this book will permanently transform their lives.

Code #7516 • Quality Paperback • $12.95

The Seven Deadly Needs
By Edward Bear

A guide around the potholes in life's road that will give you directions toward a better life. The seven chapters contend with the everyday issues that confine rather than expand our experience of reality. These obstacles keep us from an awareness of how rich our lives can be. Through the course of the book, you will learn how to overcome these deadly needs, how to see the possibilities open to each of us, and how to view each day as a wonderful opportunity for living.

Code #7761 • Quality Paperback • $9.95

NEW BATCHES OF SOUP
TO NURTURE THE SPIRIT

Chicken Soup for the Golden Soul

This collection of timeless wisdom has been especially selected for those sixty and over and others young at heart.

Code #7257 • Quality Paperback • $12.95

Chicken Soup for the Christian Family Soul

An inspirational collection that will fill your hearts with Christ's love.

Code # 7141 • Quality Paperback • $12.95

Chicken Soup for the Teenage Soul III

The long awaited third volume of *Chicken Soup for the Teenage Soul* offers teens more life lessons and heartfelt stories from their peers.

Code # 7613 • Quality Paperback • $12.95

Chicken Soup for the Writer's Soul

These tales are guaranteed to inspire every writer . . . and every reader who is a writer at heart.

Code # 7699 • Quality Paperback • $12.95

Selected titles are also available in large print, hardcover, audiocassette and CD.

Available wherever books are sold.
To order direct: Phone — **800.441.5569** • Online — **www.hci-online.com**
Prices do not include shipping and handling. Your response code is **BKS**.